Illuminate
You Are The Light Of The World

Radiate
You Are A Star Right Where You Are

Resonate
You Are A True Work Of Heart

Copyright © 2016
All rights reserved
Cover design by Sam Ashworth/Lynda Simon
Author's photo Ann Marie Walts
ISBN-13: 978-1530234998

ILLUMINATE RADIATE RESONATE
is dedicated to the ones I love:

My entire Poole, Bearinger and Jetton families,
especially my beloved husband Dr. Max T. Jetton,
for *preaching* the truth "You Are The Light of the World."

My L'Oreal USA ~ REDKEN 5th Avenue NYC
and professional industry friends ~ you know who you are,
for *teaching* me the truth "You Are A Star Right Where You Are."

My lifelong global and ORPAC/Molalla friends ~ you know who you are,
for *reaching* out with the truth "You Are A True Work of Heart."

And to Lynda Simon without whom this book would
never have arrived into your hands.

Contents

	Preface	Pg 7
1	Illuminate -You Are The Light Of The World	Pg 19
2	First You Go To Michigan	Pg 23
3	Then Journey Down Ohio Way	Pg 39
4	And Send Him Off To School	Pg 47
5	The Unfolding Story	Pg 65
6	And Then Another Bundle	Pg 73
7	Following The Call To Beavercreek	Pg 81
8	Now When The Next One Came Along	Pg 91
9	Janet Marleah Brought With Her A Love So Pure	Pg 99
10	Radiate -The REDKEN Years	Pg 117
11	Beautiful=Be You To Full	Pg 133
12	Radiate -You Are A Star Right Where You Are	Pg 139
13	Body Radiates	Pg 149
14	Thoughts Radiate	Pg 155
15	Relationships Radiate	Pg 165
16	Finances Radiate	Pg 195
17	Spirit Radiates	Pg 207
18	Resonate -You Are A True Work Of Heart	Pg 219
19	The Transition Of REDKEN	Pg 231
20	Manhattan To Molalla - A Journey of Faith and Love	Pg 243
21	Isaac's Story	Pg 253
22	The Double Life Of The Pastor's Wife	Pg 259
	Epilogue	Pg 261

Preface

"With God all things are possible". Matthew 19:2

This scripture is the promise that was framed and hanging on my wall in my 502-square-foot New York apartment, affectionately dubbed "The Pod" by my dad. The plaque has been a part of me since I can remember, first adorning the home of my mother's parents, the Bearinger's in Michigan, then my home where I grew up and now my adult home. It's promise has been lived through these lives of my grandparents and parents, and now, thankfully through me.

I do believe it. And there is one major life regret that even God could not make possible because of my pride and stubbornness.

I don't dwell on it as a major life regret, but if I did, it would be that I allowed pride get in my way of getting a book published over three decades ago rather than accepting a co-authoring gift that was offered.

Johnny Bench - Hall of Fame baseball catcher, rated one of the greatest living baseball players of all time, suggested that we co-write a book on the themes of "nothing's impossible through positive living." That was 1978.

In the late '70's, Johnny had just published his autobiography "Catch You Later" and we became acquainted through a series of serendipitous events.

My father had four daughters, and always said, "I got my girls at the hospital, and I'll get my boys at the altar." Growing up with him and his intense interest in playing and viewing sports made my sisters and me avid sports fans even to this day.

To be sitting with Daddy on Saturday nights, chomping on popcorn and watching the fights (sponsored by Gillette, "to look sharp and to feel sharp too....") was the best hour of the week for me. As a young, enthusiastic pastor, the needs of the church members took much of his time and attention; so to be with him in where we could view sports was my cherished time with dad.

Being raised in small towns near Cincinnati baseball was spelled R E D S. We were itinerate fans. I grew up in the era of Gus Bell, Joe Nuxhall and Roy McMillan playing at Crosley Field and was thrilled when the Big Red Machine of the 70's with Johnny Bench, Pete Rose and Joe Morgan made their historic mark on major league baseball.

Why or how it suddenly came to me in 1974 that I wanted to meet Johnny Bench, I don't know. Perhaps because he played baseball, was single, successful and handsome? I can remember saying a prayer that went something like, "Lord, you created Johnny Bench and you created me so I know it's no big deal for you to get us together. I'm asking and believing it will happen." And I let it go.

It was just a matter of days while working at Designers' Loft Salon in Dayton, one of our clients, Sue Lilly, arrived for her appointment. Sue looked at me from across the reception room and squealed, "You're perfect!" I thanked her and then asked, "Perfect for what?"

"We're having a benefit downtown this week for a little boy who has leukemia and we've invited Johnny Bench to come and emcee the event. Several of us will go out for breakfast afterward and I wondered if you'd like to go."

Would I like to go? Of course! It was the first time I was fully conscious of a specific prayer, that I prayed, was answered.

I drove to the event in the Winters Bank Building and there he was. We met. I felt like I was in a dream. Following that meeting there were other meetings in Los Angeles, in San Diego and Cincinnati. These produced many wonderful conversations. Johnny felt my focus on positive living and he called one beautiful day while I was living in Thousand Oaks, California. This was the hometown of Sparky Anderson the manager of the Reds and a great place for them to rendezvous and play golf. It was during that phone call Johnny presented the idea that we write a book.

Tapping into his contacts in New York, we'd get a ghostwriter to help us. Then we'd go on a speaking tour to promote the truths in the pages and tell the experiences of our lives - he a kid from Binger, Oklahoma and me a preacher's kid from Dayton, Ohio.

My one life's great regret is that I didn't accept his offer then and there. No! I had to butt in and suggest that I try my hand at writing it - to which he agreed - the gentleman that he is.

That was 37 years ago.

This manuscript, my meager manuscript, was held prisoner in various incarnations in my head, in a dozen different file folders, and on computer files. Occasionally I'd release it 'on parole' in mini-forms through handouts in the global training sessions I presented to groups of salon professionals or in magazine articles and interviews.

Fiery determination to "finish it for sure this time," following motivational seminars I attended - like the fire walk with Tony Robbins, a "See You At The Top" meeting with Zig Ziglar, or a 'writing /yoga conference' at Kripalu Retreat Center in the beautiful Berkshires.

For whatever reason, I was immobilized. The book sat alone and unfinished. I'd beat myself up if I chose to do something else other than sitting at my computer adding to and refining the book. I'd go home at the end of the day and channel surf until all hours to lose myself in the varieties of television programs; or I'd spend an entire Saturday at the gym or yoga class; or I'd become so engaged in my work, family or romance that I was just too busy to give the quality time and energy to its completion.

Sound familiar? Has procrastination ever held you hostage to that which you really know needs to be done, and yet it seems to always get the back-burner treatment?

I can only imagine what might have happened if I had taken Johnny's original offer and had the book finished in 1979. But one thing I've learned these past 37 years is to accept "everything's perfect, and I'm grateful."

Here's why I believe that.

On the perfect fall morning of September 11, 2001 at around 8:30 a.m. I was finishing my daily devotional reading and prayers in my apartment in New York City. At the time I was connected to a wonderful man who'd called me from his home on the fourth fairway of his golf community. It was our ritual to greet the morning with each other and before hanging up he'd remind me to "stay safe on the streets of New York today." I promised I would.

It was now 8:45 a.m. I began gathering my things and headed to my office at 47th Street and Fifth Avenue. Hearing a plane overhead I thought "They must be coming in low into LaGuardia (airport) today." Never mind. I said my morning greetings to the best doorman in the world, Frantz, and Jimmy our faithful maintenance man.

Strolling up to Fifth Avenue was a joy. The day was simply beautiful. I stopped at the corner at 3rd Avenue and turned into the sun rising over the East River to absorb its brilliant light filling my body, mind and soul. In my head I sang a little Sunday school song;

"A sunbeam, a sunbeam
Jesus wants me for a sunbeam;
A sunbeam, a sunbeam
I'll be a sunbeam for Him."

By the time I arrived at L'Oreal headquarters at the corner of 47th I noticed the whole population of busy New Yorkers on Fifth Avenue looking southward. The taxis, normally zigzagging their way and honking through the traffic, were peculiarly calm; the walking traffic stopped on the sidewalks. Everyone's eyes were focused on the World Trade Center Towers down at the tip of our Manhattan island; they were in full view.

World Trade One was spewing smoke and flames. Oh what great memories of this place immediately flashed for me. I recalled the times the breathtaking view of Manhattan from the famous Windows on the World restaurant would be "oohed and ahhed" by all of us - family, friends, colleagues. We enjoyed each other's company basking on the Five Star service, gourmet food and entertaining music.

I remembered many special dining experiences at "Windows on the World" located on the 107' floor with my REDKEN colleagues who traveled from all over the world to enjoy the cuisine and the view of the greatest city on the planet.

I also reflected on the weekend of my 25th REDKEN anniversary celebration in 1990 when my parents traveled to New York to surprise me and join in the celebration planned by my colleagues. We had attended Marble Collegiate Church on Sunday morning and enjoyed brunch serenaded by gospel musicians.

We were that much closer to Heaven

It was perfect.

So many memories of that beautiful place. Now I was watching as smoke continued to encircle Windows.

Back on the Avenue, my colleague Maria Cerminara jumped from a taxi at that moment startling me with the words, "On 10/10 Win news they just reported a plane just hit the World Trade Center." I stood there with Maria. Soon another colleague Cedric Fort approached us. Looking at the shock in our faces he said, "What's wrong," and we turned him around to face the blaze.

At that moment, a ball of fire burst through the second tower and there was a collective gasp of all standing with us….men in yamakas women with shopping bags, business people with computer cases. A young woman behind us on a cell phone yelled out, "I'm a newlywed and my husband is down there. He just called to say he's ok." She burst into grateful tears. Taking her - a perfect stranger into my arms - I thanked God for this one spared.

Later I questioned myself, "When would I have EVER hugged an unknown New York woman on the street?" The answer is "Never!" But this moment wasn't like any moment I'd ever lived. Every moment since has been unlike any other. We were all profoundly changed.

I made my way into my office building walking and dialing my cell phone at the same time. I had to call now. I wanted to make contact with my mother and daddy to let them know what I'd just experienced.

"Mother, turn on CNN," I cried. "Something terrible has happened at the World Trade Center."

"Honey," she sweetly said. "I've just been reading this morning in Jeremiah 31:3 where he said, "No matter what's going on, God is in charge." As always her calm resolve soothed my troubled mind. I took this as my prayer for the day. "No matter what the drama is going on around me, God is in charge," over and over I'd repeat this promise to myself.

As the events unfolded, surrealism turned to reality and reality into fear. Along with most of the REDKEN employees, I was dismissed to go home and immediately was glued to my television. Up until 3:00 a.m. that first night, all day on Thursday well into the early morning of Friday watching every news report and image that CNN could prepare for instantaneous broadcast. I grew to appreciate the sincerity of the anchors and the fearlessness of the reporters. I especially found solace in Aaron Brown in New York. The way he reflected for even a moment on the completion of a story moved me - he was feeling our pain and disbelief and sharing in the moment.

My own fear increased. Though I answered countless phone calls and e-mails with the promise, "No matter what's going on God is in charge," and added to that, "Love casts out fear," I was reminded of the human unsettling this experience was giving me. I was a mess.

There was also the realization that I couldn't know what part of this experience God was in charge of….but one thing I could do. I could choose to put God in charge of me! And it was from that place that I was able to go into action with those who were closest to me to do what I could to bring peace to their world.

I know that Love and Fear cannot dwell in the same space at the same time. So I was determined to Love everyone and everything with which I was faced. Whenever I was faced with my own fears, I realized it was because my focus would have returned to ME. I knew better. I know when the trials of life surround like a cloud, to go into service. That always takes the attention away from self and puts it onto someone else.

I couldn't do everything, but I could do something.

My colleague and friend, David Stanko, had been displaced from his apartment in the Wall Street area. His one desire was to have some peace and comfort of home; clean sheets, towels and to take a shower in a bathroom that wasn't swathed in dust. Though my place is small, I offered my pullout couch, dinner of Chinese food up on my roof garden and a long, hot, cleansing shower with fresh, fluffy towels. He accepted my invitation. And I felt that I was contributing to the chaos by giving one New Yorker a peaceful experience.

Another colleague Sam Mattingly was displaced without her closet full of beautiful clothes. I was moved to go to our Ann Taylor store in the street level of our lobby and pick up a few choice things that she could feel fresh in....not abundance, but thoughtfulness. That was the order of the day.

A great moment of gratitude was the evening of the 11th, when I was convinced to get ample provisions into my home. We didn't know at the time what other unforeseen attacks might still be coming, so having our homes stocked with food, water, supplies was a good idea.

I walked the two blocks to my local grocery to get the things that I thought would be nutritional and comforting at the same time. I was loaded down with six full bags when I stopped to wait for the light to change on Second Avenue.

Down the Avenue they came, like a military convoy, the skilled workers of Con Edison, my power company. Counting "twenty-three, twenty-four, twenty-five" trucks loaded with cables as big around as my arm, cranes, and spools of wiring.

"How wonderful, that even in the midst of conflict, there was a plan in place for disaster." There were people available and trained, supplies ready to be dispatched and everyone knowing their responsibility when they arrived on the scene.

At that moment I was grateful to be a customer of Con Edison. From that night on, every month I was grateful to write the check for the use of power in my home.

By Saturday, my loving family decided I needed to get out of New York City and have a few days of R & R in Ohio. My sister, Tot and her husband Sam came to my rescue driving twelve straight hours from their home near Cincinnati, to pack me up and take me home. I was so thrilled to see them pull up in their van in front of my apartment building. We hugged and cried together.

I wanted to share with them a bit of our experience, so we walked the two blocks to my local fire station where we stood in silent homage to the ten brave firefighters that were not going to return to the house. Candles, flags, flowers, cards took their solemn space out onto the sidewalk and passersby's stopped as we did for a moment of tribute and prayer.

After dinner, we packed the van and began the return trip to Ohio, delivering me to the safe harbor of my parents.

Home!

We arrived Sunday evening around 8:00. The neighbors came out to greet us; kids came running waving American flags. I felt like a returning war hero. For the next week I allowed myself to receive the tender loving care of my family and friends.

The outpouring of faith in our country's resolve was broadcast worldwide, something I never thought I'd live to see. The unified members of Congress singing **"God Bless America"** on the steps of the Capital; Billy Graham at the National Cathedral, the Prayer For America service from Yankee Stadium. I sobbed when Bette sang **"Wind Beneath My Wings"**. We were reminded by one of the ministers "We will get through this." I wept when Dan Rather, CBS News anchor, broke down during his visit on David Letterman's show while reciting the verse of Katharine Lee Bates' **"America the Beautiful"**:

> ***"Oh beautiful for patriot's dream that sees beyond the years***
> ***Our alabaster cities gleam, undimmed by human tears."***

Dan followed that quote with the startling reality, "We can no longer sing those words, our city's gleam was dimmed by all our tears."

Blessed is the nation whose God is the Lord, Psalm 33:12.

As Julia Roberts admonished all of us to "love one another, God is great," tears flowed.

The words of strength and power from our President Bush - "this is a battle between good and evil, and make no mistake about it, good will overcome," from our Governor Pataki referring to those who lost their lives - "they would be proud." The words of resolve and hope from our Mayor Guiliani - "We will rebuild and we will be stronger"- all those words were life giving to me during those days.

When the mayor bravely looked into the camera on Saturday Night Live and spoke the words, "Our hearts are broken….but they're beating," I felt a powerful force shoot through my body and knew it was time to resume my life.

I made plans to return to my New York, to board an American Airlines flight, and to walk back to my office on Fifth Avenue, Monday morning, the first of October.

On the evening of my first day back, following my routine walk from the office to Sports Club LA in Rockefeller Center, I gasped when I turned down the block that led to the promenade.

The flagpoles surrounding the rink were ordinarily filled with the flags of all the countries or of some special promotion at the Center. That night they were proudly waving American flags. I'd never seen that many flags in one place at one time. The scene literally took my breath away. Under my breath I sighed, "I love my flag. I love America."

After my hour workout and steam, I left the club and walked across Fifth Avenue at 50th Street, the windows of SAKS Fifth Avenue were strangely demure. Thinking they had pulled the blinds and were changing the fashion themes, I had to look twice. Beautiful sprays of white flowers of every description filled gigantic vases bathed in white light in the corner windows. Every window background was painted black and the single message printed in white lettering across the bottom of the window spoke for all of us, "with sadness."

As my eyes turned from the windows, I mustered up courage to take my first real look down Fifth Avenue. Instead of seeing the lighted windows in the Twin Towers holding the fort at the base of our island, there was emptiness. I was immobilized. "Where are the Towers?" I lamented. Again my tears flowed.

The next morning another beautiful fall day, I approached the office and looking down the Avenue, I was empowered by what I saw. Never again the familiar sight of the World Trade Center Towers, but what I saw was sky! Tiffany-box-blue sky. I immediately began singing,

> *"Blue skies smiling at me,*
> *Nothing but blue skies do I see;*
> *Blue days, all of them gone,*
> *Nothing but blue skies from now on."*

From that moment on I had a new inspiration of the horrible tragedy. Before 9/11 I would stand at the corner of 47th and Fifth - the 575 building and proclaim we were "the center of Fifth" as the bronze plaque on our building declares.

To my left I could see the towers of the World Trade Center representing the treasures of the world being traded every day in the free enterprise system we so often take for granted. Those who took them down believed the way to destroy an ideology was through destruction of its "temples." Little did they realize that capitalism doesn't live in a building, capitalism lives in the hearts and minds of Americans. For me the towers were icons representing REDKEN's theme of "Earning a better living."

To my right were the icons representing REDKEN's theme of "Living a better life" with that of SAKS Fifth Avenue, St. Patrick's Cathedral, Central Park and the Metropolitan Museum of Art. They are icons of the temples of the soul. Those responsible for the destruction of these material temples didn't count on the fact they could not destroy the temple of the American Soul.

At the center of Fifth we were helping salon professionals learn better, so they could earn better, so they could live better. And then the Towers were gone. I could no longer use them as the visual icon.

When I saw the blue sky it then became clear to me that sometimes the goals and dreams I have for my life were like the Towers. Set in my ways, set in my determination, set in my focus, I only saw the towers ahead of me.

Now that they were gone I was forced to look up, to see blue sky. This meant that now my life was about not knowing what's next, not having a clear vision of where I'm headed or what's on the agenda. Simply trusting, looking upward and living each day in the Divine "I don't know" broke my addiction to always needing to have the answers.

All of these experiences, and many more, moved me to finally finish and self publish my first book, GET GLOWING: You Are A Star Right Where You Are.

That September morning was just another morning when those citizens of our city were just going about their lives, doing what they do, loving those they loved, earning a living, living their lives. The one burning question I've asked myself, "What would they say to me right now if they could?" "What would they advise me about any indecision or problem, anxiety or worry that I have?" When I take time to sit in stillness I can almost hear their voices saying, "Do it now!" "Don't worry, be happy now!" "Love now!"

It is out of honor to those who died to reaffirm our country's faith and freedom that I retrieved this manuscript from my head, out of the file cabinets and the computer. I did it for the firefighters from my neighborhood station Engine 8 Ladder 2 on 51st Street between 3rd Avenue and Lexington. For our 565 Fifth Avenue building security guard, George, whose uncle was not found, and George came to the gruesome conclusion, "He must be there 'cause he's not here."

And I wrote for my friends and colleagues Brent, Diego, David and Mark who made it through fully alive yet displaced from their apartment homes that at one time enjoyed a magnificent view of the World Trade Center.

It is now that I write Illuminate Radiate Resonate with even more clarity of purpose as I hum the song my mother recited to me to accompany her promise, *"I have loved you with an everlasting love."* Jeremiah 31:3

> *"Oh joy that seekest me through pain*
> *I cannot close my heart to Thee;*
> *I chase the rainbow through the rain*
> *And feel the promise is not vein,*
> *That morn shall tearless be."*
> George Matheson

I
ILLUMINATE
You Are The Light Of The World

This is the story of my family tracing the dedication of a shy, reticent boy called into the ministry and the 24/7/365 demands of the pastorate in Southwestern Ohio during the years of 1943 through 1986; my mother the pastor's wife and mother of four daughters who also lived true to her "calling" by contributing her talents for 30 years in the public school classroom; the daughters educated beyond high school, three with college degrees, two with masters degrees, one with a nursing degree; among them nine marriages and six divorces; three babies born out of wedlock; incarceration on felonies of theft and drug dealing; an attempted suicide; an abortion; eating disorders; two adoptions of children followed by reunions years later; sexual dysfunction; adult attention deficit; survival of California earthquakes and fires, and the attack on New York City's World Trade Towers on September 11; lives lived on disability checks and food stamps; breast cancer; an ALS (Lou Gehrig's Disease) diagnosis; Crohn's disease requiring double amputation, death in the recovery room; pacemakers and shoulder replacements, sudden death ~ sudden glory.

And through it all, celebrating! Always celebrating holidays of every kind especially the big ones; Thanksgiving, Christmas and Easter, Mothers and Fathers Day; Birthdays, Graduations, Weddings, Anniversaries, baby dedications, retirements and new home open houses.

The stories told here are sometimes told through the transcribed spoken and written words of my father, mother and us four daughters each of us born to nurture our faith and unique gifts while living in the "fishbowl" of the parsonage.

All in all, during our growing up years, the church became the center of our lives - home life, social life, educational life. This was the Church of the Nazarene, its roots solidly in the Wesleyan tradition, evangelistic and hopeful. "Holiness Unto The Lord" was the mission then, and now. The vital modeling the girls received from their folks was written beautifully in these lyrics by Helen H. Lemmel:

> **"Turn your eyes upon Jesus, look full in His wonderful face;**
> **and the things of earth will grow strangely dim,**
> **in the light of His glory and grace."**

A best friend is something that a pastor and his wife rarely are privileged to claim due to the shadow of favoritism that could rear its ugly head. In our parents' experience, there were four best friends including computer corporate executive Ralph and Ruth Hodges, fellow pastor and elder in the church Virgil and Virginia Applegate, church pillars Herald and Imogene Wilson and Harold and Ruth Reinhart. Mother's closest confidantes were her sisters who were also wives of pastors, Fonda Dickerson, Naomi Ballmer (both now in Heaven with Pauline), homemaker Mary Hasemeyer and school teacher Janet Knotts.

The churches we pastored, the homes we occupied, the programs we presented, the evangelists who came and went all colored our view of the world through the eyes of Faith.

Our material needs came through the "food poundings" where the church members would come to the sanctuary and roll the canned goods down the center aisle as a show of loving support, the Christmas gift envelope filled with a cash gift. The Sunday School picnics, Easter egg hunts and the farewell potluck dinners made for relationship building and wonderful memories.

Our up-close-and-personal exposure to foreign lands through the messages and artifacts of visiting missionaries stimulated the girls' wanderlust whether dreaming of opportunities to travel internationally or domestically in the family car on summer outings. Daddy was a lover of history and on those travels he'd insist on stopping at every historical marker along the journey. When we returned to our school textbooks, We 'd most assuredly see in print the very places we'd visited.

The sanctity of marriage was beautifully modeled by our parents. Mother would urge us to "find someone just like your daddy" to be our life's mate. Often the loving couple would get caught stealing a moment of affection prompting a disgusting, "Eeeewwwww" from one of us.

Finishing the kiss, one of them would look at us and respond with the obvious question, "Would you rather see us fussing?"

The dream of getting married came early on as we were eye witnesses to the beautiful brides in flowing wedding dresses. Attending the reception, filling up on cake, creamy mints and salted nuts, watching bride and groom open their presents and finally joining in the celebratory "throwing of the rice" convinced each of us girls that getting married was a beautiful affair and something we definitely wanted to plan in our future.

Then there were the funerals. At an early age we came in direct contact with grief as we witnessed the tears of family and friends standing at the casket viewing their loved ones' motionless body. Following the memorial service in which Dad officiated by singing, praying and speaking a message of hopeful condolence, we attended the family gatherings. Oh how we just wanted to play yet knowing somehow play was not appropriate on these occasions.

Professionally, each of our lives was invested in service in a wide variety of worlds; public school education, professional beauty and nursing. Through these avenues we continued our folks' 'ministry' as they had nurtured us, **"Train up a child in the way they should go and when they are old they will not depart from it."** Proverbs 22:6

And through all these experiences ~ the joys and sorrows, the happiness and sadness, the growth and loss, the successes and failures, one message was believed, lived and shone through loud and clear in the lives of our dad and mom. It was the song mother would request our "dream quartet" sing every time we were together.

The lyrics by John W. Peterson were taken from the final verse of Psalm 23, **"Surely goodness and mercy shall follow me all the days of my life, and I will dwell in the house of the Lord forever."**

To know my life intimately, and to understand the full-circle journey of faith and love in which I've been privileged to live, move and have my being, I first reach into the rich heritage from which I came, both genetically and spiritually. A Chinese proverb quoted by Thomas Jefferson, comes to mind,

"To forget our ancestors is to be a tree without roots, a river without a source."

Through this journey we will see how THE Light of the World illuminated the hearts and minds of our family members through our tree roots and river source. Through faith and prayers for literally centuries, we are privileged to share the truth, You Are The Light of the World.

2
First You Go To Michigan

In their third pastorate out of college, following an associate position in Ft. Wayne, Indiana and lead pastorate occupying a six-car garage in Wauseon, Ohio, my 27-year old parents moved to Hamilton, Ohio, in the Southwest corner of Ohio just 39 minutes from Cincinnati.

To stimulate the church faithful and open the doors to potential converts, they hosted the "poet evangelist" George Hilton Talbert to preach a week-long Revival. This was the fall of 1949.

Filling his time in between preaching duties, "Brother" Talbert penned a poem telling the history of Wes and Pauline and the development of our family. You can almost hear him read it, sweet and sing-song-y, as they sat around the pre-revival dinner table:

> *First you go to Michigan the land of deer and otter*
> *And stop at Preacher Bearinger's for his second oldest daughter...*

> *The one with all the charm and grace and heart as big as Heaven*
> *Rare beauty and the kind of faith to lift, bless and leaven.*

> *Then journey down Ohio-way and find a man named Poole*
> *And get his son named Wesley and send him off to school*
> *To meet the preacher's daughter and fall in love for sure*
> *And give them full salvation with hearts made clean and pure.*

> *Then take them to a parsonage and let some time roll past*
> *Where love grows rich and deeper to tie the love-knot fast.*

> *Then right down from Heaven a bundle comes one day*
> *To bless and light and gladden their upward pressing way.*

There you have the recipe, I hope it's not a muddle
Just Wesley K. and Pauline Poole and Toddikins the puddle.

And then another bundle, according to God's plan
A sweet and chubby bundle, they called her Little Ann.

Now when the next one came along, they surely wanted HIM
But he turned out to be a girl, they called him Cathy Lynn.

Janet Marleah brought with her a love so pure and sweet
Pauline's dream to have a girl's quartet was perfectly complete.

First you go to Michigan the land of deer and otter
And stop at Preacher Bearinger's for his second oldest daughter...
The one with all the charm and grace and heart as big as Heaven
Rare beauty and the kind of faith to lift, bless and leaven.

My mother, Pauline, was the second born daughter of Clayton Anderson and Ada Almeda "Meda" Bearinger. Her life in the parsonage began in the womb as her father was a "home mission" pastor, the planter of new churches on the Michigan District all the while she was growing up.

Clayton Bearinger had a remarkable life story as told to Pauline who captured them in her book, "Now Abideth Faith."

Jeannette Farnham Anderson had been in earnest prayer by her little hair trunk in her bedroom of her humble home, and as was her custom, she always sang a hymn as she arose from her knees. These were dark days. She leaned heavily upon the Lord, for she was now in her ninth month of pregnancy for her tenth child, and she had been widowed two months before when her husband, David, had died suddenly of a heart attack. This particular morning she expressed her testimony with this blessed song, *"My Faith Looks Up To Thee"* by Ray Palmer:

> *"May Thy rich grace impart*
> *Strength to my fainting heart*
> *My zeal inspire*
> *As Thou has died for me*
> *O may my love to Thee*
> *Pure, warm and changeless be*
> *A living fire!"*

Jeanette had a royal heritage having descended from the Lord Farnham family in Surrey County, England. The Farnhams were English. The name came from two words, fern and home or "home among the ferns." They were farmers in Surrey and Midland counties.

Farnham Castle is one of the oldest landmarks in England. For years it was the home of the Bishop of Winchester. It first was the fortress in the troublesome time of Henry du Bois, the brother of King Stephen and Bishop on Winchester. It was taken in 1216 by Louis, the Dauphin, but captured and restored to the see (Church of England) in 1218. In the reign of Henry III, it was partly destroyed, but soon afterwards was rebuilt.

Today it is the Centre for International Briefing, established in 1962, and has the longest history in delivering intercultural training. It serves highly tailored and interactive blended learning solutions designed to provide international personnel, in every function, with the required skills, knowledge and tools to develop both general and culture specific intercultural business skills.

Lord Farnham was a prominent figure in the history of England during the War with France.

Ralph Farnham came to Boston in 1635 on the ship, the "James" after an eight-day voyage. The Farnhams were brave, grand soldiers and fought for our country during The Revolutionary War, the War of 1812 and the "Great Rebellion."

Tall, muscular, fair-haired, blue eyes, intelligent, apt and active, they ever manifested the "blue blood" which was in their veins. Their motto on the family coat-of-arms was, "Hollis addictus jurare verba magistri" which translated reads, "Inclined to swear in the words of no master."

General Lafayette (Gilbert du Motier, Marquis de Lafayette), the French aristocrat and military officer, fought for the United States in the American Revolutionary War.

When he was in our country, General Lafayette declared "the Farnham women of Andover, Massachusetts the most beautiful women on this side of the Atlantic Ocean."

In honor of this family, with whom he stayed for many weeks, he wore the "Golden Fern" worked with silk in his neckerchief.

From this lineage came Benjamin Franklin Farnham who settled in Bucksport, Maine. At twenty-one years of age he left Maine and settled in New Richmond, Canada. There, in 1838, he married Katherine MacNeil. The youngest of their six children was Jeannette Louise Farnham, the mother of Clayton.

David Anderson, father of Clayton, came from Inverness, Scotland. He loved music and made violins when he was not occupied at his task as a blacksmith in the little village of Lum, Michigan. To David and Jeanette were born nine children. Each child shared the responsibility of survival in their near poverty existence. David had been converted to Christianity just a year before his death.

On February 4th, 1885, during a severe snow storm, Jeanette gave birth to twin boys. Assisted only by a mid-wife in the Anderson home, her delivery was very complicated.

She gave her life for her babies.

A local pastor, Rev. Alva Phelps, came to the aid of now eleven orphaned children. Two of the older children were able to care for themselves, but nine were placed in foster homes.

The pastor was acquainted with a couple who lived on a farm close to the Anderson home, Bill and Barbara Bearinger. In their early forties, they'd never had children of their own. Rev. Phelps spoke to them explaining the desperation and asked them if they could take the newborn babies.

As much as she wanted to be a mother, Barbara felt overwhelmed with the thought. She felt incapable of taking both of the boys. Going to their knees in prayer, the Bearinger's ultimately agreed they would not adopt both. They chose Clayton, he was four days old.

His twin Clinton, adopted by another Christian family in that small town, had a short-lived life; he died within six months.

When Barbara and William took Clayton to their home his only clothes, lovingly sewn by the ladies of the church, were packed in a tiny wooden chest that David Anderson had made from scraps of wood.

No child could have been more loved by his new parents or by the pastor and people of the church. Pastor Phelps would often take him to the platform of the church and pray prayers of thanksgiving and blessing on this "treasure" that had been sent to their friends.

Clayton grew up with the "family altar," listening to his father and mother voices lifted in prayer as part of his daily schedule. The Bible was always open on the kitchen table where it was read each morning before the farm work began.

Church attendance was never neglected, including mid-week prayer meetings, and quarterly meetings even though they had to travel by horse and buggy to the church several miles away. Every Sunday morning they attended Sunday School and the morning service, returning home to have a meal, take care of the farm chores, and then travel back for the evening service.

As soon as he could talk, Clayton played church always using his little "Testa Book," a New Testament written for children. It was a gift. From those early imaginings, he began to yield his young heart to God's calling.

At the age of nine, when Clayton was climbing a cherry tree, the limb on which he was standing broke, he fell painfully straddling a lower limb. This injury resulted in an abscess requiring emergency surgery which took place on the kitchen table. The Bearinger's, Rev. Phelps and others gathered to pray over the medical attention Clayton was being given.

A true miracle of healing took place that night. The following Sunday, the physician and pharmacist who provided the surgery and antibiotics, arrived at the Bearinger home. They found Clayton sitting at the parlor organ singing **"What a Friend We Have In Jesus."**

During the winter of that same year, a religious revival was being held in the Owen Church, east of Lapeer. The Bearinger's, wrapped up in coats and blankets, traveled in their horse-drawn buggy. They had faithfully attended services every night for two weeks.

One night Clayton felt a deep conviction, a stirring in his heart and mind. He remembered the Bible text, Matthew 11:28, **"Come unto me all ye who are heavy laden and I will give you rest."** That night he confessed his sins, was converted and his name written down in the Lamb's Book of Life. He became a child of God and the seed of faith began to grow.

The little country school played an important part in Clayton's early scholastic training. Each day he would walk nearly two miles to the Bearinger School. One-room was filled with children of varying ages and grade levels. His dedicated teacher did her best to teach the Three R's ~ Readin,' Ritin', 'Rithmatic.

In her heart, she knew many of them would never be able to continue their studies in high school.

One day during recess, Clayton's playtime was replaced with devastation through one of the older boys who ran up to him egging him on in a teasing voice:

"Bearinger's aren't your real parents, Bearinger's aren't your real parents."

This came as a complete shock to him. Over and over the words played in his head, "Bearinger's aren't my real parents?"

When he arrived home from school he ran to his mother and asked, "Aren't you my ma?" Holding him tightly, wiping his tears, Barbara told him the story of his adoption. She summed it up with one statement.

"You are our son through love and Divine providence." Her soft voice soothed his confusion. It was all he needed to hear, all he needed to feel. He never questioned his place in their lives again.

As prosperous farmers in the fertile Michigan soil, the Bearinger's spared nothing when it came to showering Clayton with everything materially he ever wanted. His wants included a Western pony, complete with a buggy and his first car, a runabout Ford. When his father presented it to him, he also gave instructions to his son, "You may go to Imlay City, but don't drive over 12 miles per hour."

At sixteen, Clayton began his preaching ministry offering sinners an altar of repentance under the arbor of a tree or a make-shift canvas tent. Clearly on a Divinely-called path starting with his early "playing church" and his conversion as a teenager, he now felt the definite hand of the Lord for the purpose his life; itinerant preaching and interpretation of the scriptures. This was his life for a full year.

Then he began to realize what he needed was a helpmate, a wife, to share in the work of the Kingdom.

Ada Almeda "Meda" Swain lived on an adjoining farm from the Bearinger's, with her parents, brother Joe and sister Leah. Her father was a deeply spiritual man who was faithful to raise his children in the *"nurture and admonition of the Lord,"* Ephesians 6:4.

Grandfather Swain was a lover of music and bought 8-year old Meda a parlor pump organ on which she was given lessons. She looked forward to gathering in the parlor to sing as her father played. His advice for Meda came directly from the scriptures, Proverbs 22:1, *"A good name is rather to be chosen than great riches."* Meda passed this down to her own seven children.

When Meda was nine years of age, her father died, and with his death her whole life changed. Her mother was not a Christian and begrudged all the times Clayton and his family would pick her up for church activities.

When she was eleven her mother told her if she was going to believe that "religion stuff" she would have to do it away from home. So at that tender age she began working as a "house girl" for a family in Lapeer.

Meda longed to attend 'normal' school to become a teacher, but with no financial help she had to put that dream aside. She continued to work in homes until she was sixteen. She stepped away from being a housekeeper to become a retail clerk in the Vosburgh Department Store in Lapeer.

During her early teen years she was enticed by a "worldly" crowd and neglected to stay close to the Lord until one night in 1916. Meda and her best girlfriend attended a meeting under one of those canvas tents. Clayton was preaching. At the conclusion of his sermon, Meda realized her 'backslidden' condition and at the altar she sought forgiveness and reclamation.

Clayton rejoiced with her over her return to the Father's house.

Believing in and acting on the scripture from Deuteronomy 32:30, *"If one can chase a thousand, two can put ten thousand to flight,"* Clayton began courting Meda. One evening while sitting together in the parlor, he on the piano bench and she on a nearby chair, he popped the question, "Will you marry me?" She shyly said, "OK."

The following year, on May 29, 1917, they were married at 10:00 p.m. after the tent meeting service at Richfield.

Meda possessed all the attributes of the ideal pastor's wife. She loved his ministry. She believed in his message. She listened carefully without interrupting him when he would share difficult times and problems with her. She made his home his castle. She protected him from having to listen to gossip. She was his prayer partner, secretary, wife and mother of his seven children for sixty-five years.

It was while they were in their first pastorate in Potterville, their first child, a daughter named Fonda was born. Just two years later, after a move to Colling, came Pauline.

As the girls grew up, they loved to harmonize while working in the kitchen with their mother or while standing for what seemed like endless hours over mounds of ironing. They began singing duets on a weekly radio broadcast hosted by a local pastor in Pontiac, *"The Happy Half-hour of Heaven and Home."* Their mother would sit in the second row in front of the girls and pantomime the words so they would feel more comfortable.

Never was there a "Divine appointment" so finely tuned than one fine day when the girls, now high school age, were invited to sing at a luncheon attended by "ladies that lunch," among them, Grace Dow, the wife of Dr. Herbert H. Dow, the founder of the Dow Chemical Co.

In 1936, Mrs. Dow established the Dr. Herbert H. and Grace A. Dow Foundation in memory of her husband. The purpose and activities of the foundation were to give support for religious, charitable, scientific, literacy or educational purposes for the public benefaction of the inhabitants of the city of Midland and of the people of the state of Michigan.

Grants were given largely for education, particularly higher education.

Following the girls' musical number and their father's devotional presentation, Mrs. Dow approached Rev. Bearinger. Within earshot the girls heard her say, "I was so moved by the message in song that your daughters presented today, I've been impressed to offer to pay their way to college."

This was a definite answer to prayer. Without the generosity of Mrs. Dow the girls had no way to finance their dream of attending Olivet Nazarene College in Kankakee, Illinois. Through Mrs. Dow they made their way to, and through, school and there they met their life partners.

At various times of the year The Lord continued to supply the Bearinger's needs through "poundings," which were showers of sugar, flour, meat, milk, cornmeal, canned goods, coffee, tea and quilts. Clayton would also assist his farmer neighbors at harvest time, hold revivals, even wallpaper the homes of his church members for additional money that was always needed for the church or his family.

Along with pastoring the Richfield and Potterville churches, the Bearinger's organized the Zion Hill church with eleven members. The combined salaries from these churches never totaled more than ten dollars each week.

Clayton possessed a winsome personality, never met a stranger, and these qualities were priceless when attracting people to the new start-up church and building a congregation.

One such memory was recounted when telling the story of a neighbor in Potterville. He lived across the street from the Bearinger's and early on let Clayton know with anger in his voice, "I hate preachers." A man of grace and inclusion, Clayton simply replied, "Ok."

The man was taken completely off guard, thinking that the new preacher in town would put pressure on him and try to convince him that preachers were good neighbors, too. To implore him to come to church. Not so.

The man eventually invited Clayton to come see the pride of his life, his rabbits. "Want to come see my rabbits?" Clayton responded enthusiastically, "Sure!"

There were over 100 rabbits, some were 22-pounds; beautiful rabbits. "I'll give one of these to your wife, but I'll *never* give one to you," the neighbor gruffly spoke.

Clayton paused and then responded, "I'm glad you're giving one to my wife; she always shares everything with me."

From that point on, the preacher-hating neighbor began to come around, eventually becoming the custodian at the church. His own faithful, believing wife had her prayers answered.

In their youthful days, Clayton's children felt there was nothing he couldn't do. He showed them how to garden, how to split kindling wood, how to build a fire in the wood stoves for cooking and heat, and how to fish. He was never too busy to take time to sing with them or to help put a project together for school.

Because Clayton's income from the church was so meager, he taught the children economics with the money they would earn from their jobs like paper routes, house cleaning, ironing and clerking in the local stores. Seldom did they ask their parents for extra spending money. They knew it just wasn't there. One of Pauline's greatest disappointments came when she approached her dad about getting braces on her irregular teeth complete with over-bite.

The good reverend looked at his lovely sixteen-year old daughter and said, "Pauline, I'd love to be able to give you braces but I just *can't*."

In addition to the scriptures and spiritual principles, there were life principles modeled by their parents and abided by the children in the Bearinger home, which now in addition to Fonda and Pauline included Bernard, Naomi, Mary, Bill and Janet:

1) Before saying anything always ask yourself, "Is it kind, true or necessary."

2) First thing in the morning make your bed. "You never know when Daddy may bring the District Superintendent home for dinner."

3) While cleaning up after each meal, the kitchen mantra was "Wash and wipe together, Fuss and fight no never."

4) "Live each day one day at a time and fill in each day with love, kindness and understanding."

Right up to their golden years, the Bearinger's desire to preach heart holiness kept their faith strong. They lived and proved the Lord's promise from Ephesians 3:20 **"Now unto Him that is able to do exceeding abundantly above all they could ask or think."**

Even this scripture couldn't prepare them for the unexpected material windfall that would come to them.

Meda's mother who had asked her to leave home at the age of eleven because she was a Christian, now was asking her to pray with her to find the Lord as her own personal Savior. Not long after her conversion, Meda's mother died, leaving her sister Leah who was stricken and bedfast due to Multiple Sclerosis.

Leah called the Bearinger's and told them she would Will her properties to them if they would move into her home and care for her. For forty-six years the Bearinger's had lived in parsonages, and now they were to own their own home.

Leah lived only three weeks after the transaction.

The "exceeding abundantly" continued to come to the Bearinger's. The general church was providing a monthly retirement check along with social security payments so that they could provide for their temporal needs on a fixed income. Again they praised the Lord for supplying all their needs.

But something greater was in store for this pioneer couple.

Clayton's own sister, Mary Anderson Voorhees, had always sent the family ten dollars each Christmas during the children's years at home. She lived in Napa, California with her husband A. P. Voorhees, the owner of a local haberdashery.

At the age of 82, Mary died after a short illness and in her Will she named Clayton as one of her heirs. All the years in home mission churches Clayton and Meda had to furnish their home with second-hand furniture. There was never a complete set of dishes, glassware or flatware.

Because Meda was an excellent seamstress, the children's clothes were homemade.

Now came cartons of silver, silver trays, coffee and tea services, crystal goblets, beautiful china and linen table cloths and napkins fit for a royal family.

British blue blood was their DNA.

Beside all of these material treasures, Clayton shared in a legacy that was to provide for them comfortably the rest of their lives. Clayton had always remarked that God had always supplied their needs. What could he possibly want?

He decided on a new car that he wouldn't have to share with the finance company. His financial independence now allowed him to endow students' education at Olivet and Mount Vernon Nazarene Colleges (now Universities) where seventeen of his children, grandchildren, and in-laws had been educated.

He continued to teach, exhort, sing and counsel as the opportunity would be presented. He felt that "Holiness of heart covered every area of the gospel spectrum, repentance, restitution, forgiveness, cleansing, growth in grace, maturity, stewardship, discipling and missions." His faith in the message was constant.

There was no time that Clayton needed to rely on the promise of holiness of heart than one night at camp meeting with the unthinkable happened.

The girls, Fonda and Pauline, joined their mom and dad at the Eastern Michigan District Camp meeting in Holland, Michigan where their dad gave his 65th ministerial report. Both Bearinger's had been in good health all winter and spring, but the week before camp meeting started, Meda became ill with the flu. She didn't respond to the medication and remained very weak.

One day she said to Clayton, "Now doesn't that beat all! I've looked forward to camp meeting all year and now I can't go to the services."

On Tuesday night, Meda felt well enough to eat her evening meal at the table with her family. Pauline shared the message that Dr. Mendell Taylor had given in the afternoon service on the portion of the Lord's Prayer, "Give us this day our daily bread."

Meda's heart was blessed and tears flowed down her checks as she praised the Lord. As the time for the evening service drew near, Clayton asked if she wanted him to stay with her.

"Heaven's no," Meda replied, "that's not necessary." He kissed her goodbye and began the short walk with his two daughters to the tabernacle.

After church, returning back to the cottage, they found the lights were out. They became curious. "Why would mother sit in the dark? She always keeps the light on for us." Clayton walked into the bedroom where he found his beloved Meda lying on her side in their bed, a one-hundred year old comforter perfectly covering her.

She had fallen asleep and had gone to be with the Lord.

At the precise time the family was hearing the great choir singing, **"Worthy Is the Lamb,"** Meda Bearinger made her entrance into Heaven.

The very next day, Sunday, during the afternoon service, Clayton sang in full voice the words of the hymn, **"How Firm a Foundation,"** expressing his testimony for a seventy-nine year walk of faith with the Lord.

> **E'en down to old age all my people shall prove**
> **My sov'reign, eternal, unchangeable love;**
> **And when hoary hairs shall their temples adorn,**
> **Like lambs they shall still in my bosom be born.**

When he finished singing, he asked for a moment of "personal privilege" and gave his testimony of God's presence in the midst of his grief over being separated from Meda. He began singing acapella, **"Amazing Grace"**. A heavenly spirit swept over that camp meeting crowd.

That was to be Clayton's last message in word and in song in a camp meeting.

A vision came to Pauline of her mother ushered into Heaven by angels. She heard the shouts of saints that had gone on before saying, "Here comes Meda!!" and Meda in her quiet reserved manner replied, "Oh, folks you didn't have to do this for me!"

Then she turned and looked at Pauline and assured her, "It's alright, dear, I'm going to help the Lord prepare for the Marriage Supper of the Lamb."

The following months were lonely ones for Clayton without Meda. He spent little time at the mobile home in Anderson. Each of his seven children had a special time for him to visit hem and enjoy their love and devotion. His final trip was to Lakeland, Florida attending a camp meeting and hearing the clarion call of Holiness, the life he had lived and proven to be sure and steadfast.

Over one hundred of his friends and twenty-one from the Flint Central Church of the Nazarene honored him at a special diner they had planned for him.

Upon returning to Anderson, he proceeded to have a cataract surgery. The night before the procedure his last words of admonition to Janet, Dave, Pauline and Wesley were, "I'm completely submitted to God's will. My message is still Divine love out of a pure heart."

The surgery was successful, he devoured his evening meal. And then, the following morning he suffered a stroke, paralyzing his left side. When Janet and Dave came to visit on Sunday afternoon he motioned for them to come to his bedside, and he stammered out the words, "I Love You."

Within minutes Clayton died. He had fought a good fight. He had finished the course. He had kept the faith in the doctrine of full salvation. Divine love out of a pure heart.

3
Then Journey Down Ohio-Way And Find A Man Named Poole And Get His Son Named Wesley -As Spoken In Wesley's Own Words

"When my maternal grandmother, Johanna Wolfe was 14 years old she traveled alone on a boat to New York City. She often said in her broken German brogue, "I came into this vorld all by myself. "

Both she and her husband George, were first generation Germans. Grandfather came over earlier. Grandma's sister was already here. They migrated to Cincinnati, Johanna and Matilda, George, Henry and Will. They lived in Woodlawn a northern suburb and once they were settled they never again spoke their native German language. "Dat's the old vorld," Grandma would say, "Dat's the old vorld."

Grandfather Ziebold, having a creative and mechanical German mind, was very talented in the use of his hands; machinery and things of that nature. When my mother, Irene was a small girl, they moved to Buffalo, New York for his employment.

Grandpa was a difficult man to live with, stubborn and strong minded. I heard Mother say many times about Niagara Falls, "I would hear the tumble of the water, but never got to see the falls." He wouldn't permit it. It wasn't until after she married, I was 12-13 years old, she made a trip to New England and got to see the Falls for the first time.

Back in Buffalo, Saturday was market day. Grandma and Mother (Irene) walked into town to get groceries and provisions. Faithful each week, the Salvation Army stood on the busiest street corner where people were coming and going. Their little band would play and sing gospel songs striking a chord in Grandma's heart. Grandma, raised in Germany, had a Lutheran background.

The two would stand by to listen to the familiar songs and hear a gospel message. The Lord was speaking to my grandmother's heart. Getting home late Grandpa always wanted to know where they had been.

On one Saturday, The Salvationists took the big bass drum and laid it down on the street corner to make an altar. Inviting people to pray, Grandma was moved by the Holy Spirit and said to Irene, "You take dese baskets and hold dem, I've got to go pray."

"Oh Mama, Mama don't do that, you know what Papa will do when we get home!" Irene pleaded.

It was at that old bass drum, on a street corner in Buffalo that my grandmother became marvelously and wonderfully saved.

Mother recalled, "There were times when we'd get home and walk into our yard filled with great maple trees. My mother would say to me, 'Irene you stay out here behind the trees and I'll go in and see how Papa is.'"

He drank heavily which aggravated his temper, his demeanor. So there were times when he'd be in a rage and would threaten the life of my grandmother.

When they eventually moved back to Woodlawn, my mother now 12 years old, became converted in a gospel meeting sponsored by God's Bible School. Grandma and mother took the Interurban to the meetings. The services were so glorious by the time they'd get back on the last car going to Woodlawn, it would be 11:00-11:30 p.m. before they got home.

Infuriated, Grandfather wouldn't tolerate their late arrival, always causing a battle royal when they got home. He'd go into raging madness, dishes thrown, furniture broken. This went on for several years. He blamed his belligerent spirit on her faith and faithful church-going.

In one of those moments, he took her by the hair and held her against the wall with a straight razor at her throat. Then came the threatening words, "Old woman, if you ever go back to that church I'll slit your neck from one side to the other."

Through it all, a great, long spiritual romance Grandmother had with the Lord and it had an influence on my mother and ultimately on me.

Grandfather's hatred turned against my mother. Stories poured out late in her life of the sexual abuse against her as she became the pawn, the reward, for the winner of the drunken card games regularly hosted in that old shop in the backyard.

One incident she recalled was when her father slapped her for professing her love for Christ. His handprint was indelibly left across her beautiful face.

"I didn't feel the sting....really I didn't. I experienced the slap, but I honestly didn't feel the sting. Christ took it away."

At 16-years old, she was forced out of the home simply because she wanted to live a Christian life. She moved out and found a tranquil, safe harbor as a housekeeper and maid in a medical doctor's home. My mother was meticulous, a marvelous cook and excelled in pastry making. On Sunday she'd go to church and see Grandma.

Within a few years, she went down to God's Bible School in Cincinnati with an inclination to become a missionary. That never developed as far as foreign overseas mission work. She sang in the college choir and enjoyed involvement in other campus activities.

She had no financial support, so again she made herself available to do housework. She was selected by the GBS president M.G. Stanley and his wife to be their maid. This gave her a great opportunity of broadening of her personality, experience and character under their influence. That is how she made her way at God's Bible School.

While at GBS my father Basil came from Henderson, Kentucky, to be a student and that's where they met.

The guidelines of the conservative school in regard to social life, boys and girls dating, were very restrictive. They were never allowed to be alone. There was always a chaperone. The "three foot rule" prevailed. If you had a boy or girl friend you couldn't be closer than three feet while on campus or in the corridors.

Cincinnati boasts its lovely parks and one day, Irene and Basil wandered off campus, alone, to Eden Park. Under the canopy of the romantic Gazebo, which still stands, he proposed to her. They married.

There were two separate families out of my grandparents' Ziebold marriage. Of the four in the older group, Mable died drowning in a cistern, another was stillborn. Three children survived and grew into maturity including my mother, Irene, Clark who became a machinist like his dad, and Henry a Godly man and a bi-vocational pastor. He, too, knew how to work with his hands in tool and die making. On Sunday and Wednesday he'd preach, start a little church then return to his 'day job' on most days. There are two or three churches Cincinnati today that were started under the ministry of Henry Ziebold. My mom and dad helped Uncle Henry by supporting during revival meetings by attending, singing, praying and giving.

Three younger children came later to George and Johanna's family. These children were living in an environment where the relationship of their father and mother wasn't getting any better; it actually got worse. Depression, not the Great Depression, but a great personal depression came along for Grandmother.

Grandfather had a shop on the back end of lot where he would escape and hone his skills in safe making. He worked for a while in Hamilton at Mosler Safe and the Herring-Hall Safe Companies. When my mother got married he made a little safe with her name printed in beautiful script that would be kept in our home for as long as I can remember. When my mother and daddy died and we took things from the house, I kept that safe and treasure it highly.

In the meantime, the little mission down in Lockland became an organized church, that's where I was raised. I remember the founding pastor and each of the pastors there on through.

I was born on 22nd October 1920 and in May 1922 I was 18-months old. The little mission building was on a lot where that the Mill Creek came down next to the church. On a Sunday afternoon, the church had a baptismal service. There was a minister from God's Bible School, Brother Finch. That afternoon, now 65 years ago, I can remember just like it happened this morning. A warm day, my father was carrying me in his arms, holding me, as a father would an 18-month old baby. He and mother wanted me to be baptized. He handed me over to Brother Finch who wore a gray tunic cut suit and white shirt that was buttoned up to the neck, no necktie. He took me down to the water and baptized me.

The house where we lived, 241 Shepherd Avenue, from the church would be not quite a mile. My brother Basil, sister Anna Mae and I were wheeled in a big wicker perambulator baby buggy with huge wheels. Our folks would put all three of us in the buggy and wheel us to church.

At the church we had folding chairs and all the little kids would dangle and swing our feet. Sure enough, the chair would topsize, hit us on the back of our heads and fall on the floor making all kinds of commotion.

When the pastor started a little orchestra my folks bought Basil a saxophone, Anna Mae learned to play the piano, and I had a little ¾ violin. We played in the services every Sunday morning and night. Tuesday night was orchestra practice night. I was about 9 or 10-years old and in all the orchestra boasted 18 different instruments.

Along about this time my grandmother had become weary of the war going on at home. The older three children were grown and had families of their own. The three younger ones Elizabeth, Virginia, and Harold "Bud" my uncle who was just a year older than I. From where we lived over in Evendale, we'd go to Woodlawn and pick up this crowd, take them to church and then drop them off. This was our life.

Many times my grandmother would visit with dad and mom after we'd get to Woodlawn. We kids would get out of the car to play because we knew they needed privacy as she didn't have anyone else to talk to. By this time, the older children had gone their various ways, so one of the issues they discussed was her weariness and she didn't need to "put up with this any longer" meaning her living situation with Grandfather.

Her plan was that each of the older children would take one of the younger ones into their home and she would divorce Grandfather. The plan was all set.

She was a great woman of prayer. Whenever Grandma prayed she looked up toward the Heavens and kept her eyes open. When the Church of the Nazarene pioneered work in Europe and Germany, General Superintendent Dr. Jerry Johnson explained about a whole group of people in southern Germany who prayed with their eyes open.

That was the way Grandma prayed.

After she made arrangements for the children to be parceled out, she made it a matter of prayer. It was after those times of real earnest prayer, she told mother and dad one night after we brought them back from church, "I've decided I'm not going to do dat (divorce George). I made a vow to God when I married my husband....'til death us do part. I cannot break my vow to God." She went back home.

Grandfather continued to drink, making his own home brew that would render him drunk. Eventually it was that alcohol and lifestyle affecting his body in a devastating way.

Today we call it cirrhosis of the liver, then it was called dropsy. He was moved from the shop into the house where Grandmother took care of him. His legs swelled like great balloons with bags of water and when the blisters broke he had no choice but to spend his days in an oversized chair with his feet and legs wrapped in towels and placed in washtubs.

When it got to the point where he needed 24-hour care, his mean disposition became increasingly demanding and difficult. Uncle Will was now staying all night, sitting up with him. One particular night Uncle Will implored Johanna, weary in body, mind and soul, to go to bed.
In the dark of the night, Grandfather screamed, "Johanna!"

Uncle Will didn't pay any attention to him.

Again, he screamed out, "I vant Johanna!" Will finally responded, "Anything Johanna can do for you I can do for you."
"But I vant to pray!"

"Now George, you've put that off (praying) for 60 years; you can put it off 'til Johanna is awake at 6:00 in the morning."

Grandfather, pushing up the sleeves of his pajamas, spit into and rubbed his hands together saying, "If that's the vay it is, I'll just do it myself." He began to pray.

Mrs. Nutley, the neighbor whose children we took to church every Sunday, woke her husband Ernie. She heard a great uproar and urged him put on his trousers. "Go out in the yard and find out what's going on over at the Ziebold's."

After a few minutes he returned to his wife. Crawling back into bed Ernie simply said, "They're having a prayer meeting."

After having a glorious conversion, Grandfather remembered early on in Will's life he'd been a vibrant believer. Grandfather remembered this and said to his brother, "Vill, you had this once and gave it up. Never, never vill I ever give this up."

That next weekend, Grandfather wanted to go to church. It was the first and only time we could recall his getting dressed up. It was in the middle of the service he stood on his bound legs and addressed the pastor.

"Brother Moore, I vant to say something. I vant to apologize to you. I've been a mean man, said bad things about you, cursed you. I vant you to forgive me."

Then he turned to his faithful wife Johanna and his children, "My family, I vant you to forgive me. And this congregation, I want you to forgive me."

He then told his story, gave his testimony, and sat down. Following church, my father delivered Grandfather back home, helped him into his pajamas, lifted his feet back into the tub.

Ten days later Grandfather died.

Grandmother reflected. "I'm so glad I didn't do what I wanted to do (get divorced). If I had done that and left him alone he would have died in that old shed with those old drunken bums and gone to hell."

4
And Send Him Off To School

To meet the preacher's daughter
And fall in love for sure
And give them full salvation with hearts made clean and pure.

Wes was a reticent, shy, backward student at Olivet Nazarene College in Kankakee, Illinois, just south of Chicago. One evening he was kneeling in prayer at the rickety desk chair in a small, upper level bedroom of a private home just off campus. This was his "dorm room ," offered to him due to limited financial resources, by his former pastor, Rev. and Mrs. C.T. Moore. This was truly a gift from God.

Downstairs, while "Sister" Moore was busy in the kitchen, he could hear her alternatively humming and singing the tune of "Blessed Assurance" and occasionally filling in the words penned by blind songstress, Fanny M. Crosby:

"Perfect submission, all is at rest, and in my Savior am happy and blessed....
Angels descending bring from above, echoes of mercy, whispers of love"

As she prepared the evening meal, Wes began to pray. The urging of the Holy Spirit led him to open the Bible to a scripture that he interpreted as the call on his life. A life of ministry. A life in the pastorate. A life in the parsonage.

Through his tears he said out loud, "Oh Lord, no! No, you have the wrong guy! I can't even put two sentences together, how do you expect me to stand before a congregation and preach?"

"Fear thou not for I'll be with thee, I will still thy pilot be…." came the words from yet another great old hymn written by Emily D. Wilson. In that humble place, in that shining moment, Wes accepted the call. He tells of "floating" down the stairs, running into the kitchen, lifting Sister Moore off her feet while kissing her cheeks and exclaiming, "Oh Sister Moore I love you. It's real! It's real I've been called to be a pastor!"

As a part of his training and to help pay for his college tuition, Wes' musical background served him well. His beautiful tenor voice blended with three of his college friends to form a quartet sent from the school to churches each weekend for promotional purposes.

These opportunities allowed him to preach often and began to hone his skills in the pulpit. Although still painfully shy when it came to one-on-one relationships and conversation, he would soon be paired with one who had all those qualities and more to be his helpmate.

Pauline was so like her dad, Preacher Bearinger. She felt a calling on her life when she was 16, when the Holy Spirit convicted her and she "felt like the worse sinner, ever."

Her conversion and life experience would be based on the scripture from Isaiah 61.

"The Spirit of the Lord is on me, because the Lord has anointed me to proclaim good news to the poor. He has sent me to bind up the brokenhearted, to proclaim freedom to the captives, and release from darkness for the prisoners to proclaim the year of the Lord's favor …to bestow on them a crown of beauty instead of ashes, the oil of joy instead of mourning, and a garment of praise instead of a spirit of despair.

She surrendered her heart's desire to perform on the big stage, a dream inspired by her father's sister, Mary Anderson Voorhees, an 'elocutionist' who performed dramatic readings on legitimate stages around the world including The Lamb's Club in New York City.

Pauline settled for a calling to perform on the smaller stage, in elementary and high school classrooms to fulfill what she felt was the Lord was imploring her to do, "Feed my lambs."

She was like her dad in one other major way, she never knew a stranger. She often said, "at the base of the cross we're all the same." This philosophy aided in her approach to anyone, anywhere to begin a conversation. At Christmas time she'd walk through the shopping mall and when approaching a young mother with her baby in tow, Pauline would say, "Looks like you already got your doll for Christmas."

The mother would giggle and admit she had the most beautiful baby in the world.

This in contrast with Wes, when he'd see a baby that didn't have what he thought were redeeming qualities, he'd simply exclaim, "Now THERE'S a baby!" Enough said.

Wes and Pauline's dating history was tepid, credited to Wes' timidity. Pauline would get exasperated with him when they'd go out and he would hardly say two words. She so wanted him to be outgoing, the life of the party, the center of attention. Wes was true to his character, allowing only the Lord to develop his personality.

They were married on the same day Wes graduated from Olivet, May 28, 1943. Graduation ceremonies were in the morning and in a quick change of the chapel in the lower level of the administration building, the wedding took place. Wes and his best man, Leslie Parrott, who returned to Olivet years later to assume its Presidency, were late for the wedding causing them to have to climb through a window in the pastor's study to enter the building. They arrive just as the bride was poised to take her walk down the aisle.

As a practical joke Wes' groomsmen spread Limburger cheese on the motor of the "getaway car" so that the fumes of the stinky cheese followed them all the way to their honeymoon train waiting to take them to Cincinnati. Their honeymoon days were spent at Wes' folks', a 5-room cottage on 1 1/2 acres, filled with apple, cherry and peach trees, grapevines, a lucrative garden, chickens, honeybees and lots of love.

They started their life together in a virtual Garden of Eden.

> ***Then take them to a parsonage and let some time roll past***
> ***Where love grows rich and deeper to tie the love-knot fast.***

Wes and Pauline accepted their first pastorate in Ft. Wayne Indiana as associates to Rev. S.E. Singleton. They soon moved to Wauseon, Ohio to take the responsibility as lead pastor for a small Nazarene congregation worshipping in a converted six-car garage.

With each move to a new congregation, the Lord always provided a teaching position in the local school system for Pauline. He was as committed to her ministry as He was to Wes and the church.

> ***Now there you have the recipe, I hope it's not a muddle***
> ***Just Wesley K. and Pauline Poole and Toddikins the Puddle***

All in divine timing, the loving couple built the Wauseon church attendance by building deep and rich relationships. One of those relationships was with a local turkey farmer whose name reflected his profession, Brother "Turkey" Jones. He loved his pastor and would do anything for them. When they found out they were pregnant with their first child to be born in January of 1945, "Turkey" committed that he would pay the doctor and hospital bills for the new bundle of joy.

And he did. On January 25th, Lois Virginia was born. It was a difficult delivery for Pauline and as a result, she was confined to her hospital bed for ten days following Lois' birth.

When Wes came into the room following the delivery he found his firstborn in the arms of his beloved who exclaimed, "Oh Honey, isn't she beautiful?" Wes glibly replied, "No, I think she's ugly." Pauline was devastated. Already aching from her birthing experience, his unthinking remark struck her heart.

Grandma Bearinger arrived from Michigan to care for Pauline and baby Lois who Grandma would endearingly bathe, change and repeatedly say, "You're my little Toddikins; my little Toddy."

The name stuck. For her entire life, rarely was she known as Lois, except in her professional education circles; forever she was "Tot" to all of us closest to her.

At twenty-three months old, Tot was featured in the Christmas program at church. While Pauline was busy around the house, particularly while ironing, she would repeat the story of Jesus' birth captured in the second chapter of Luke.

Tot's bright mind and natural desire to perform prepared her to repeat the story, word-for-word without a hitch on Christmas Sunday to a full-capacity at the small Millville Avenue Church of the Nazarene, now the third pastorate of the Poole's. The small tyke stood tall on the church platform and began reciting word-for-word,

"And there were in the same country shepherds abiding in the fields keeping watch over their flocks by night;
And lo, the angel of the Lord came upon them, and the glory of the Lord shone allllllll around them, and they were sore afraid.
And the angel said, "Fear not for behold I bring you good tidings of great joy which shall be to all people.
For unto you is born this day in the City of David, a Savior which is Christ the Lord.
And this shall be a sign unto you; you will find the babe wrapped in swaddling clothes and laying in a manger."
And suddenly there was with the angel a multitude of the Heavenly host praising God and saying, "Glory to God in the highest, and on earth peace and goodwill to men."

Tot excelled in everything in which she participated at Fillmore Elementary. With her long, blonde finger curls she was cast as Goldilocks in "The Three Bears."

She was selected to recite "The Night Before Christmas" in the school holiday program, she was a star and she loved the atmosphere of school.

When Tot was in the fifth grade, dad accepted a call extended by the Nazarene church in Bethel, Ohio, a small town of 2,500 just 38 miles east of Cincinnati. Throughout her years in junior high and early high school, Tot was popular and elected to leadership in student council, cheerleader and girls' chorus.

All of us loved Bethel. Mother found her niche in Bethel High School teaching English. In those days, she would begin each class period with a scripture reading, prayer, and the Pledge of Allegiance to the flag. Her open Bible on the desk was a silent witness of her faith to all who entered her room. The teenage boys and girls who were influenced to attend our church through her invitation included the five starters on the Varsity basketball team, the Homecoming Queen and court, and others who held leadership positions in the student body.

During her duration as high school teacher, she was nominated by the students, faculty and parents for the "Treat Your Teacher" recognition award sponsored by the Cincinnati Post-Times Star newspaper. We were so proud of her, sanctified pride of course, when her photo and biography was printed in the newspaper. A local celebrity, our mom.

After church on Sunday evenings, although we had little space in our cottage parsonage or money to host them, the kids would flock to our house for pancakes or waffles, potato chips and Pepsi. They loved being together and loved being in the home of their pastor and his wife.

My sisters and I gloated in the fact that the basketball team hung out at our house. When the Bethel Tigers made it to the county championships, we painted signs and carried pompoms to the game, cheering out loudest to root, root, root for the home team. We cried the hardest when they lost, too.

Two of those boys actually moved into our home and became family. First was Walt Murray who was living with his grandmother and had a penchant for frisky risk-taking like putting cherry bombs in the urinal in the high school. He had a sweet heart and a softness to romance. Walt came to live in our home his senior year.

Our second "brother" was Carl Eddie Haslam. Our dad loved sports and wanted to show his support of the local high school teams, football and basketball. On a Friday football game, Carl Eddie suffered an injury to his back. Daddy saw it happen and after the game he went to check on the young 15-year old Sophomore.

What he found was not to be believed. Carl was living alone in a one room apartment in the upper space of a home. The only available light came from a single light bulb dangling from the ceiling in the middle of the room. With the exception of an older sister he had no family.

Daddy came home from the visit with the burden on his heart to invite Carl to come live in our home and be a part of our family. He asked Mom about it and her response, "I'll have to pray about it."

She did and the next week we made room in our small parsonage for this natural athlete, moving from football to basketball and taking the Bethel Tigers to a County Championship. Carl attended Bowling Green University in Kentucky and then headed to Florida where Walt Disney was designing a new amusement park. He achieved his master electrician certification and spent months into years underground Disney World and Epcot in making the connections that would keep the place functioning.

Although Jerry Earles didn't live in our home, his mother and sisters were faithful members of our church in Bethel. He was a young "snot- nosed" kid who attended Sunday School reluctantly and did what he had to do to stay on the Varsity basketball team. During the championship game, Daddy walked into the locker room at half-time and saw Jerry on his knees, 'Oh God, Oh God, PLEASE let us win!" Once Jerry was puffing away on a cigarette and he caught Dad's eye.

 Stuffing the lighted cigarette in his front pocket it continued to simmer while Daddy kept him occupied in conversation. He never smoked again. Jerry chose to enter the Army following graduation from Olivet and became a military chaplain. If our dad had pride it was sanctified, and he was most proud of Jerry.

Harry Fulton, another member of that basketball team, lived next door to the church in an abandoned county jail. He was the primary caregiver for his Aunt Nan who was confined to a wheelchair. Harry was a star student, athlete, and natural leader. Mother recognized his gifts and encouraged him to further his education.

"There's just no way," Harry responded to her. "We have nothing. I'd never be able to afford to go to school."

And then tragedy struck our little town of Bethel. The Deitz family owned the local furniture store. They had a son, David, who was much like Harry, a born leader. One night David was killed in an automobile accident. In his devastation, Mr. Deitz came to my parents with an offer that was Divinely earmarked for Harry Fulton. "We've saved for David's college education all his life, and now he's gone. Would you know of a worthy student that we could support in sending to college."

That worthy student was Harry Fulton. He chose Olivet, graduated with honors and continued post-graduate work until he finished his Ph.D., returning to teach at Olivet for years. He was a business major and the quest of putting into practice the theories he was teaching the college students, he opened his business and became wildly successful.

Each of these boys, and more, were a part of Mother's influence in the classroom and Daddy's influence in and out of the pulpit.

During the summer she loved making the trip to northern Ohio to St. Mary's and the Nazarene District Youth Camp. On the campground she found delight in working in the campground cafeteria, attending the chapel services and developing her personal relationship with God.

Tot also developed a personal relationship with a preacher's kid from Cincinnati. They were crazy about each other and though the miles separated them during the school week, he was faithful about driving to Dayton to visit on the weekends.

Until. The big until was a new pastors' family moved into our district, first as evangelists and then as pastor of a church in the suburbs of Cincinnati. The proximity of the new pastor's eldest daughter to him. She was beautiful, cheerful, bright AND could play the piano! A major plus in those days.

Tot took the demise of her relationship with him terribly hard. A small, blue stuffed puppy dog toy that he had given her, which she named "Torry" - the combination of their names, was the only remnant she had of her first true love experience.

Daddy had now accepted yet one more call to the 'big time' in church talk, to Dayton where dad took the reins at the Knollwood Church of the Nazarene. This band of believers was led predominantly by Frank and Mary Morgan, pillars in the Parkview Church of the Nazarene, who moved out to the outskirts of Dayton with their family, Frank, Don, Bob, and Dorothy. Frank was an astute businessman and real estate developer.

It was on a plot of land where he found an old, abandoned dairy barn. He felt the Lord's nudging to envision a transformation of that barn into a church and make it happen. And he did. We would boast in the fact that the balcony of our beautiful church was once the hay mount, the basement housing the cattle feeding troughs.

The Morgan's attracted great people of faith into the charter membership. They were also well educated, talented and possessed superb taste. From our former home in Bethel it was definitely a "movin' on up" experience. The church bell tower would broadcast instrumental versions of hymns on Sunday morning. The fellowship hall housed a full kitchen, something we'd never seen before, a church with a kitchen!

However, when our new church friends discovered that we were coming from a town not far from the Ohio River, they referred to us as "river rats," which affected the confidence of Tot, now a 15-year old sophomore in high school.

Tot's move from Bethel High where she was popular and constantly in social demand to Beavercreek High where she was a virtual unknown, was painful to the point of almost more than she could bear.

Day after day, during lunchtime, she'd take her lunch into the girls' restroom and hide in a stall to eat, be alone and be sad. By the time junior and senior years rolled around, she had made a few close friends, mostly relying on her sisters and church friends to fill in the gaps.

There were no leadership roles, no cheerleading. She attended school, came home, was a dutiful daughter until she met Doug Lambert.

Doug was the only son of Ed and Marjorie Lambert, a strikingly handsome couple with social status, membership at the Walnut Grove Country Club and a successful automobile business. Their home was within walking distance of the high school in a newly developed 'plat.'

Because of his dad's business, and his mother's style, Doug drove the nicest car always decked out in the latest fashions. He walked with a slight swagger that matched his aura.

Tot began dating Doug in her senior year, through graduation and into her first semester of college at our folks' Alma Mater, Olivet. He remained at Beavercreek High to finish his senior year. It was during her first Christmas break that the unfathomable happened and wouldn't be revealed until Easter Sunday in the Spring.

The church at Knollwood was thriving. Executives from National Cash Register, Wright Patterson Air Force Base, Champion Paper, General Motors/Delco and Chrysler were being drawn to the ministry through the music and the message. Young families mixed with 'saints' worshipped together. Attendance was up, giving increased. God was blessing. Daddy was in his prime, just 40-years old, enjoying the fruits of his labor of love.

On Easter Sunday morning, I couldn't help but notice that Tot had taken her car early heading somewhere I did not know. Our family dressed in our Easter finery and made our way to the church for what was to be the highlight of the year with a lily-drenched sanctuary, choir in full voice presenting the Easter cantata, and everyone leaving with a box of candies compliments of the church board.

Half-way through Dad's resurrection day sermon, Tot slipped into the pew next to me. A stark look on her face and I somehow immediately knew without being told. She was pregnant.

The day crept by. We ate our traditional Easter dinner around our dining room table with all of mom's beautiful china, crystal and silver. The room decorated with lilies we brought home from the church which we donated in memory of our departed loved ones. It was as normal to everyone but Tot and me.

As was tradition in those days, the church was open for service on Sunday nights and as could be expected the crowd would have thinned down due to our congregation celebrating the day with their families near and far. Dad led the service reminding all of us that "the same power that brought Jesus out of the grave is available to us as His believers whenever we call on Him."

Never would he, in a million years, know that he would need to rely on that promise from the Bible more than ever when he returned home that night. As we readied for bed Tot asked to see Mom and Dad. My heart was pounding as I stayed in my room on the other end of the house. She met them in their bedroom and calmly spoke the words, "I'm pregnant."

Mother cried out "no!!!!" then fainted. Dad was stunned. Tot cried. The whole event is a blur now, but it seemed that within a few short hours a plan had been created to salvage the image of my dad's position in the community, church and on the district; to withdraw Tot from Olivet after the spring term (when she would just begin to 'show') and send her to Grandpa and Grandma Bearinger's home in Lapeer for the duration of the pregnancy.

Mother's teaching, our school experiences and the ongoing work of the church would be shaken to their foundations. As a family, we had to depend on each other more than ever, especially after Dad reported to the church board the truth about Tot. The response from the chairman was, "How can you expect to teach us how to raise our children when you can't even control one of your own?"

This moment was the devastating blow to my father's ministry. Through it all, he never lost his faith but that accusation crushed his heart.

For me, at 17-years old, the startling truth of my sister's pregnancy made me determine that I would never bring shame to my parents, to decide that having a baby was not a joyful experience, and to 'close my legs' to the possibility. To that end, when I was 24 I made the decision to have a tubal ligation, to have my tubes tied, my permanent solution to birth control.

Tot returned to Olivet for the spring term and packed her dorm room to return home for a for a family vacation before heading to Michigan for the final 5 months before her baby was to arrive. We made the drive from Dayton to Portland, Oregon for the world-wide General Assembly of the Church of the Nazarene. Tot was always the one who'd get car sickness on any journey, much less one that took her cross-country in June with no car air conditioner AND pregnant. We were constantly stopping along the way to alleviate her discomfort.

Our trip across America was also dotted with stops at nearly every historical marker and monument we came across. Dad loved history and wanted us to be able to look in our school books at pictures of Mt. Rushmore, Yellowstone's Old Faithful, Mt. Hood, Grand Canyon, etc., and be able to say, "I've been there!" "I've seen that!" He was so good that way. And this trip allowed us to do just that.

Returning from two glorious weeks together, we unpacked the Pontiac and repacked with all that Tot would need for her 'nesting' in Lapeer. Grandpa and Grandma welcomed her with open arms, cared for her, prayed with her and loved her through the grueling final weeks and days.

Mother's sister Jan was married to a wonderful guy, Dave Knotts. Their home in Anderson, Indiana became a touchstone for the Bearinger's in their final years. Dave's cousin was unable to have children. They so longed for a baby. Jan knew this and proposed to Mom and Dad that they consider adopting the newborn out to them.

The legal motions were set in place, the plans for adoption on the day of birth were finalized. In October of 1964 a beautiful baby girl was brought into the world and given, temporarily, the name Tot had chosen for her, "Marta Dawn. " It was soon changed to "Cheryl" by the bubbly new parents.

Mother took the baby in her new bunting and presented her to them, Daddy prayed a prayer of dedication and blessing.

Tot never saw nor held her baby.

Her delivery wasn't that dissimilar to the one her own mother experienced with her. It took many days of sitz baths at Grandma's before she felt normal. The emotional wrenching, the mental anguish she suffered far outweighed the physical pain in her body. Through the years, Tot never knew who the parents of her daughter were. We all knew but were sworn to secrecy. Talk about painful.

When we would see Jan's daughter Kim standing in a Vacation Bible School photo, or at a family reunion with a beautiful dark-haired girl, just her age beside her, we knew it was "MD."

Doug took off for the Marines and Tot returned home to Dayton. Daddy's admonition to each of us girls was, "If the bottom drops out, you can always come home." So, she took him up on that promise and moved back home.

She became a part-time student at Wright State University. Tot desperately wanted to continue her education and realize her lifelong dream of returning to the public school atmosphere where she shone as a child.

And then Doug returned home from the Marines.

Their reunion resulted in a small church wedding and reception planned in Middletown where our folks had accepted the call to pastor. She was lovely in her ivory lace knee-length dress. Her long hair in an up-do was held with a puff of netting. She carried calla lilies.

I stood with her as bridesmaid, my boyfriend Randy stood with his best friend Doug Lambert. My father united this couple so that their second baby, Heather Dawn would have a solid home.

They returned to Olivet in great style driving Doug's Mustang Shelby with baby in tow. There Tot was able to finish her degree and we made the trip to Kankakee to celebrate graduation day.

Their marriage was unpredictable. Doug was in and out. After a period of time, Tot decided once again to return to the folks' with little Heather to provide a more stable environment for her.

However, the magnetism these two had for each other was so overwhelming that within two years they reconciled, established a home and presented their third daughter to the world, Lesley Jeanette.

Lesley was the most beautiful baby. By this time I had made a decision to have tubal ligation which would make it highly improbable that I would ever become pregnant.

After all we had experienced regarding pregnancy and babies, since I was sixteen years old, my mind was totally made up. No matter what, I didn't want to get pregnant, put my body through the changes and lasting effects, nor be a mother, totally obligated to another human being for their lifetime. No babies for me.

When Lesley came along (named after my dad Wesley and my middle name Jeanette), I concluded that the Lord knew I was never going to get around to having a child and He gave Lesley to Tot for me.

As a small child, perhaps three-years old, I would say to Lesley, "Whatever we want to do, we'll do!" "Wherever we want to go, we'll go!" "Whatever we want to say, we'll say." These three chants were our bond.

Doug and Tot provided a home for their two beautiful daughters. She began her teaching career and mingled it with community service by getting the local school involved in giving back; recycling projected, environmental tree planting project, Veterans projects. She was fully in her gift and loving every moment.

Three years flew by and baby Shannon Nicole was born. Now the parents of three girls at home, it became just too much for Doug. When Shannon was three, he left them. Walked out. Took off for parts unknown. Divorced Tot. Remarried….again and again.

Tot, brokenhearted but totally undefeated, took on the role of single mother. Holding down a full-time teaching position took her days, the girls were her focus at night.

 As much as Daddy, Mother and I could help in the expenses that were now growing with growing girls, Tot knew she needed to bring in additional income to support them.

She turned to World Book Encyclopedia sales as a safety net. She was a born sales person. This was way before the internet, computers and Google, and every home that had a school-age child, would need to have the latest edition of World Book. As a teacher she understood the importance of research and growing a child's wisdom of the world through pictures and words. This job helped to fill the gap.

Theatre, since her first "performance" of Jesus' Christmas story, Goldilocks and "The Night Before Christmas" was her true love. As she matured it wasn't as important for her to be on stage, after all she was performing each day in her classroom. This time she took on the role backstage supporting the performances in local productions.

At one point, she applied for and won the position of House Coordinator for La Comedia, a local dinner theater in Miamisburg. It was here that she met one of the actors, David Schultz.

To my parents' chagrin, David and Tot moved in together at Daddy's old home place "Down Home" with the three girls. There was running water but no indoor bathroom, only an outhouse that was dreadfully scary and freezing cold at night. The plentiful foliage around the house provided shelter for the mice that would find ways into the warmth of the house and scurry their way across the kitchen floor.

Tot's warmth in decorating and providing a safe harbor came through the touches she put all around. The one great benefit was that she would be closer to her school making her commute less time consuming. David was working at a scrap metal company in Middletown, his commute a bit longer.

They were making ends meet, committed to each other and decided to get married.

A small church wedding with Doug, a smaller family-only ceremony at my parents' home, now in Fairfield, with Daddy officiating. His desire was to see Tot settled in a relationship that was loving and safe.

Heather, now 8 years old, shed uncontrollable tears just before the ceremony began. It was a foretelling of her anguish and the anguish her mother would have being married to David. The inevitable happened. David left. Husband #2 had abandoned this family of girls and never looked back. The shirking of his responsibilities left us to pick up the pieces of broken hearts and broken home. Daddy and Mother stepped in to support.

The girls said farewell to "Down Home" and returned to Middletown finding a lovely rental home, three bedrooms, one bath (for four women!) at 409 Glen Lane. A huge oak tree in the front yard provided a kind of "shelter from the storm" and sitting on the front porch made it picture perfect. It was a great location for proximity to schools, parks, church. They would feel at home here. 409 is still their touchstone of love and peace.

Community involvement in Middletown was a fulfilling way for Tot to heal through various activities, chief among them MIDFEST. A fall festival focusing on a specific country each year. The chosen country would send representation of the art, food, music, performers to Middletown and the community and surrounding area would respond with great attendance and financial support.

It was through her association with MIDFEST that Tot met Sam Ashworth, a historian, artist, graphic designer, photographer, visionary, musician and father of three. Sam and his friend Jack Howard agreed to join Tot in a project that would bring Shakespeare to the classroom, the elementary classroom, using Tot's lesson plans as the foundation for the book, "The Bard for Beginners." The three formed Globe Three Productions.

"The Bard…." was innovative in that it gave children a well-rounded view of Shakespeare and the era in which he wrote; they would learn history, science, reading, writing, art. It truly was a Divinely inspired work and sits today in the Library of Congress and the Globe Theater in England.

Sam and Tot formed more than a business relationship and he became more familiar with the family, all of us, over time. Ultimately, he moved into 409 and much to my parents' chagrin, set up house with Tot and the girls. We loved Sam, we all loved Sam.

But for our folks, living together without being married was not acceptable in the eyes of God or theirs. Many of Tot's choices were not acceptable in their eyes. I often wondered if these conscious and subconscious choices of guys and lifestyle and were her way of rebelling against her heartbreak, the move from Bethel to Dayton at that crucial time in her life or any number of other disappointments she experienced. Who knows. We'll never know.

The Ashworth~Schultz~Lambert 'gang' were always involved in planning and executing events in Middletown. They created many deep and lasting relationships. People would respond to their invitation to 'get on board' and they did because they wanted to be around Tot and Sam.

Their network grew and when it came time to celebrate the girls' graduations from Middletown High, Tot's graduation with her Master's Degree from Miami University or Sam's latest exhibition installment at the Historical Museum, their friends would come out in droves to support them.

Never was this so evident than the evening of their wedding with the site appropriately selected, The Sorg Opera House built in 1891, in downtown Middletown.

Nearly 750 family, friends and well-wishers filled the theater to capacity as Tot and Sam said their vows (Daddy officiating) and then turning the auditorium to a banquet hall and the stage to a dance floor for the reception orchestrated by their daughters.

It was sometime during the reign of Sam~Tot that she was convinced it was time to tell Heather, Lesley and Shannon the whole story of her relationship with Doug and that they had a full-blood sister.

5
The Unfolding Story
Strength For Today And Bright Hope For Tomorrow

It wasn't until Cheryl was 19, long-lanky and gorgeous that the reveal was scheduled.

Cheryl longed to become a model; had done some work in the local markets in Indianapolis and had complied a look book, a major requirement for anyone wanting to enter and approach agencies in the Big Time in New York City. I had become acquainted with leading agents through my work at REDKEN and my Aunt Jan knew this.

One day Aunt Jan called to tell me Cheryl wanted to make a trip to New York and meet me which, we knew, would open the door for reuniting her with Tot and our family. Once she found out who I was and why I was willing to help her, she then would get to meet her mother for the first time. I had to be convinced that it was time for both her and Tot for the reveal.

I agreed. Cheryl and her boyfriend arrived in New York, I met them at the Sheraton and we visited agencies. Christmas was approaching and an appropriate time for their reunion being planned by Mother and Dad, now living in Fairborn.

The house was decorated for Christmas the traditional way with a live Christmas tree, tunes playing on the stereo, the printed sign "Jesus is the Reason for the Season" was unfurled on the front yard, and colorful lights outlining the front of the house and in the evergreen trees. Dad loved Christmas and did his utmost to make the Holiday the most festive.

The doorbell rang. Cousin Kim was standing there as Mother opened it and she introduced Cheryl to her Grandmother and then to her Grandfather Poole. Behind the wall standing in the kitchen with a bit of trepidation, was Tot. Mother turned, and said, "And Cheryl, this is your mother."

They both squealed and ran into each other's arms. They cried. They laughed. They were reunited and it felt so good.

As they sat around the luncheon table beautifully decorated and enjoyed the meal Mother had so lovingly prepared, Tot couldn't take her eyes off of her stunning daughter. Reaching out and taking her hands, she examined every finger and thumb. This was the first time she had been able to see her child and she wanted to absorb as much of her as possible. The parting was sweet and they promised to stay in touch.

In the meantime, 'back at the ranch' in Dayton, Doug had returned home for Christmas and caught wind that Cheryl and Tot had been together. He was adamant that he, too, wanted to meet their first-born. With his relentless maneuvering he found out Cheryl was working the graveyard shift at a Waffle House in Muncie, Indiana.

Jumping in his car, he made the 2 ½ hour drive to Muncie arriving around 2:00 a.m. and found a seat in a booth inside the warm restaurant. The aroma of waffles, bacon and coffee filled the atmosphere and eventually a long, lanky, gorgeous young lady approached him. "I'll have coffee, please," were the first words he spoke to his daughter as he laid his eyes on her for the very first time.

When Cheryl returned with coffee and to take his food order, Doug suggested that she sit down with him.

She was stunned and wondered why this perfect stranger would have the nerve to ask her to take a seat. She quickly responded, "I'm not sitting down with you, I'm working!" Doug looked at her intensely and said, "I said sit down!" Cheryl was adamant and defied him once again, 'I'm NOT sitting down in this booth with you…..who do you think you are, anyway?" Doug responded, "I'm your father."

In sheer disbelief, Cheryl went immediately to her manager and explained that the man sitting in the booth with the cup of steaming coffee was her biological father whom she had never seen. She asked if it would be all right if she sat with him for a while. She was granted permission.

They talked and drank coffee well into the early morning hours.

The revelation of Cheryl's existence to Heather, Lesley and Shannon was something only Tot could do. She sat them down at the round kitchen table and simply said, "I need to tell you something. You have a full-blood big sister. Her name is Cheryl and she lives in Muncie."

Each of the girls made their way from Middletown to study at Miami University in Oxford and Ohio University in Athens. Heather chose education, Lesley sports performance and Shannon a path to become a dietician. Their mother continued her own education and received her Master's degree in Gifted Education the same graduation march line as Shannon and taught the SCOPE program at Adena Elementary in the Lakota school system of Westchester.

In the fall of 2003, Tot was on the telephone and when asked her name she was unable to form "Lois Schultz."

She called me in New York, "There's something wrong with my tongue. I couldn't say my name today."

Chalking it up to being tired and pulled in a thousand directions, we thought no more about it, until she began to experience carpal tunnel symptoms in her hands and arms. For several months she wore a Velcro brace on them and it seemed to give support and relief to the constant ache.

I was vacationing in the Dominican Republic at an all-inclusive resort when I received a call from our sister, Jan. She told me Tot had a diagnosis of a "chronic, but not fatal medical condition" and wanted to have a family pow-wow to reveal the diagnosis and our plan of action. Getting from the Dominican to Middletown, Ohio in neck-break speed was not going to happen, but I arrived as soon as I could. We met at our folks' home and within a few moments of arrival I found myself sitting in the floor with my dear sisters and Tot began to tell reveal the findings.

"After many batteries of tests, the doctor has presented the findings and has concluded that I have ALS, Lou Gehrig's disease. Normally it begins in the torso of the body and spreads to the limbs. Mine has begun in my tongue, they call it, bulbar palsy."

We were silent. She continued. "Sam and I have already made the decision to do whatever necessary to delay the inevitable. Eventually it will take over my entire neuromuscular system, the brain no longer getting message to the nerves and I'll lose all use of my arms and legs. Talking, if you can imagine for me, will be increasingly difficult to form words, swallowing is already becoming an issue. Breathing will be labored."

Bravely, without flinching, she asked us to believe with her the words from our family's signature hymn, **"Great Is Thy Faithfulness"**. "Please pray 'Strength for today and bright hope for tomorrow.'"

With that, Daddy began to pray and we all held hands. At the conclusion we sang in beautiful harmony, "I'll be loving you, Always....Not for just an hour, Not for just a day, Not for just a year, but Always."

Shannon had been living in Santa Barbara following the completion of her program and designation as registered dietician. Lesley was in Atlanta having followed her dream to work as a trainer in the 1996 Olympics. They decided that Shannon would move in with Lesley, Tot would join the holistic campaign they were waging against this most creepy of diseases.

A local naturopath/chiropractor put her in a hyperbolic chamber, feet in tubs to draw out the minerals from her body and offered all he knew and the girls kept their mom on a regimen that was monitored almost moment by moment.

While living in these close quarters, Tot took a calendar and marked the days when Lesley could conceive for her first child. In the midst of all her own medical issues, she was creating a new vision for Les and her husband Jay Hatfield. Sure enough, Lesley followed the X marked on the calendar and within weeks confirmed she was indeed pregnant.

While the days arrived and departed, every moment was precious to this mother and her daughters. Heather would call daily from Boston to lend her love and support. The ravages of ALS ignored the painstaking efforts. Eventually Tot would be admitted to a hospital for the insertion of a feeding tube as her ability to chew and swallow efficiently was becoming dangerous. Choking was the major concern.

Shannon, with her research into the proper nutrition to maintain her mother's strength, concocted a "smoothie" filled with everything vital. Three times a day Tot would hear the buzz of the blender and, in the earlier days, would have the capability to insert the syringe, filled with green smoothie, into her feeding tube.

She was so brave.

Within a year, she became weaker, first starting with her neck unable to support her head and requiring a neck brace. Then her legs, weak but not frail, began to buckle. Sure enough, her breathing needed support and it was determined the best way for her to survive would be to sever her vocal chords and insert a ventilator tube, hooked to a machine that would never be turned off. The vent was her lungs; the feeding tube her dining room table

Now, unable to speak, we acquired an iris-activated computer that would respond to her eye movement in spelling out words in order to communicate. This was a short-lived effort as her eyes would get weary quickly in trying to keep them steady, laser-beamed on the letter and just spelling a word was frustrating her to tears.

She was now in a hospital bed in the upper room of their lovely Tudor home in Middletown. It was roomy enough for all the equipment she needed to survive plus a large overstuffed couch where Sam would catch as many minutes of sleep through the night, when he could, and sit with her during the day.

The TV, music system, bathroom, all within a comfortable space. For this we were grateful.

When Tot had something to say, she would blink or raise her right thumb, the only moving parts on her entire body now. Thumbs up, all's well. Thumb motionless, not good.

Sam created an alphabet board we could hold and spell out words she wanted. Tot would blink when we arrived at the correct letter. This letter-by-letter "dictation" was her only means of communicating.

At the end of Christmas day in December of 2006, after she had been able to be carried downstairs in her wheelchair and sit at the family dinner table, open presents and enjoy the moments, albeit tethered to a portable vent, she indicated she wanted me to get the board, she had something to say.

We were now back up in her room, she was dressed for bed, exhausted from the day. However, she mustered up enough strength to blink out the following message.

"I M D O N E."

She was ready to go. She no longer wanted to live in this prison of her own body. She no longer wanted to rely on a machine or tube to keep her alive. She no longer wanted to have to have her mouth stuffed with absorbent cotton to capture her saliva. She no longer wanted to keep her family in captivity. It was over. She was done.

Two days before the Hospice doctor was called in to administer her vent removal, I was with Mother and asked her if she wanted to spend a few last minutes with Tot. She thought about it, prayed about it and then responded, "Let's go."

We took the final drive over to Tot and Sam's home just within a couple of miles of Heatherway Drive. We spoke very little. Mother had decided she would not be a part of the family gathering around Tot's bed two days hence, and she knew this would be the final time she would see her "little Toddikins the puddle."

Mother's weary legs took her step-by-step up to the second floor "suite" where Tot lay motionless in her bed. With each step Mother prayed, "Lord help me - one, Lord help me - two, Lord help me - three" counting the ten initial steps to the landing. Taking a breath and mustering courage she continued, "Lord, help me - eleven." Finally reaching the top of the stairs I escorted her into Tot's bedside, pulled up a comfortable chair as close as I could get it. Mother reached out and took Tot's left hand.

Stepping away and through the door, I waited in the hallway just outside. Although I wasn't in direct earshot, I was able to hear Mother's prayer. "Lord, when Tot was born we dedicated her to you. She's always been yours. And now, we return her to you."

Mother kissed her hand, and her cheek, said goodbye and headed toward me. As she got closer she said, "It is finished. I'm ready." And she made her way slowly down each stair praying as she descended. "Lord help me...."

On January 13th, 2007, I was standing next to one of Tot's nurses and friends when she looked down at her hand and then directly in my eyes. Again her eyes went to her hand and the "mom ring' that she wore on the index finger of her left hand. It had been a gift from Ed Lambert, gold with an inlay of her birthday stone, Garnet. One Christmas Tot had the ring duplicated for Heather, Lesley and Shannon. They faithfully wore their rings in honor of their mom and to feel the connection with her every day.

Her nurse spoke, "Tot, is there something about the "mom ring?" Tot blinked. She looked at me.

"Do you want Annie to have the "mom ring." She blinked again and again and again. At that moment, I knew the responsibility she was passing to me in the form of the "mom ring." I was ordained the surrogate mom to her girls.

Her nurse took Tot's hand, slipped the ring off and placed it on my hand. I cried and fell on my knees. "Oh Totty, I'm not worthy to wear the "mom ring."

She blinked, "yes" again and again.

Within moments, sixteen of us gathered around her bed. Her four daughters, Cheryl, Heather, Lesley, Shannon, their husbands, and children. Her sisters, niece, the Hospice doctor and nurse by her side to administer the treatment that would allow her to be taken off the vent.

We sang songs, **"Always"**, **"Great Is Thy Faithfulness"**, **"Amazing Grace"** and **"Do Lord"**. The monotonous sound of the vent machine was turned off. Now there was nothing but silence. We waited. The doctor continued to monitor her pulse and slowly her strong, loving, creative heart began to slow.

Within just a few minutes he looked up at us and said, "She's in Heaven."

I was standing at the foot of the bed at her lovely feet, freshly pedicured. She always wanted her toes to be freshly polished. Especially today as she prepped to leave her earthly body and step into the Heavenly realm.

The moment I heard the doctor's gentle declaration I imagined that I could see her soul taking off and her always-excited voice exclaiming gleefully, "WHEEEEEEEEEE! Free at last, free at last, Thank God Almighty, I'm free at last."

Tot was just 12 days shy of her 62nd birthday.

6
And Then Another Bundle, According To God's Plan, A Sweet And Chubby Bundle, They Called Her Little Ann

The folks have told me over and over of my birth night, January 30, 1947, in Wauseon, Ohio. The location in northern Ohio brought some of the most treacherous winters and this night was recorded as the having the worst ice storm in the history of the county.

Daddy described it as a "crystal palace" as he drove ever so slowly on the slippery and dark road leading to the hospital. Mother's water had broken just as they were sitting down to their favorite meal, meatloaf and mashed potatoes. I made that one critical move that started the birthing experience, for me and for mom.

When they arrived at the hospital they discovered that it was so dangerous outside that the nurses couldn't get from their nurses residence across the property to check in for their evening shift, it was 7:00 p.m.

Mother's doctor also had called to say he wouldn't be able to make it and a young, Army doctor who was new to the hospital, was on duty. It would be he that would bring me into the world.

The electricity throughout the hospital went off due to the heaviness of the ice on the power lines. The doctor didn't know where to locate everything he needed for delivery and made the decision to postpone until hospital staff could power up generators and get the lights and equipment reinstated.

In the meantime, I was more than ready to leave the cramped space of the womb. The doctor instructed, "Pauline, cross your legs and pant like a dog." I suppose this was the first form of what we know now as Lamaze. Mother did as she was told and kept me from pushing through until the recorded birth time of 1:35 a.m.

Due to the duration of my time in the birth canal, my malleable head was pointed and mother was concerned about brain damage. She was reassured the next morning, when they delivered me to her for my morning feeding and she saw my head now normally shaped, that I was just fine.

When it was time to check out of the hospital and take me home to the parsonage as the newest "PK," our friend and pillar of the church, "Turkey" Jones showed up and paid the doctor and hospital bills in full.

I have no recollection of that big house in Wauseon that served as the parsonage for the now expanding Poole family. Because it was in my ninth month of life that we were packed up and moved to the third pastorate, Hamilton Millville. Tot was two years and five days older than me.

We took residence on 416 Alberton Avenue, a quiet side tree-filled street with kids living up and down. Our house sat in between the Bitter's and Mrs. Yaekel. Each Christmas she would be so kind to bake anise cookies for us. I can still smell the aroma and feel the warmth of her kitchen as we bit into the hard crunch of those German-inspired red treats.

Across the street lived Dr. and Mrs. (Carole) Garrett Boone, the county coroner and private physician with their daughter Ginny, three years older than I. Ginny was a bright young girl who was rarely without her "snoodle," her version of a security blanket. "Snoodle" was three large 3" safety pins hooked together which she would rub under her nose when reading a book, watching television, or going to sleep.

Tot became good friends with Donna Bitter leaving Ginny and me to pal around. She was very inventive constantly creating "productions" in the basement of their home in which each of us would be cast. A clothes line was strung from one post to another with an army blanket to create a curtain. When it was time for the show to begin, the curtain was lifted. Our favorite production was "Peter Pan" with Ginny in the title role, Tot as Wendy and I played Tinkerbelle. I recall one time she learned the lyrics and tune for "If I had wings like an angel, over these prison walls I would fly….." I don't recall that the song was linked to any particular story.

My earliest memory of Alberton Avenue and Ginny Boone was climbing up the ladder stairs into the attic where she found an old pair of scissors.

"Go over to your house and ask your mommy if I can cut your hair."

I'd do anything Ginny asked me. My little chubby legs ran as fast as I could across the street, opening our screen door and then immediately turning around and running back to Ginny's.

"Mommy said it would be OK."

My first lie. Ginny picked up that pair of scissors and began chopping my bangs. The more she chopped the more my stomach began to twist into knots. I knew when I returned home I'd be faced with telling the truth. I didn't want to go home.

When I finally walked into the house, Mother took one look at me and said, "WHAT DID YOU DO?"

"Ginny wanted to cut my hair and I told her you said it was OK."

Mother explained the lie I had told and immediately took me into the bedroom to kneel beside her bed and ask Jesus to forgive me. This would not be the last time this activity took place. She then took me by the hand and marched me to the local barber shop. It was here I experienced my first salon visit.

The barber had a straight board he placed over the arms of the big, porcelain barber chair and mother told him to "do whatever you need to do to fix these bangs." When he completed the job, my bangs were less than an inch and very, very straight.

Being the only daughter of a wealthy doctor, a dad who read Time Magazine and sat in a large leather chair at the end of his busy day, Ginny was given anything her heart desired. Including beautiful clothes. She was a source for my sisters and me to have quality school clothes, albeit handed down.

My most favorite was the dress she allowed me to wear for my piano recital when I was in the second grade. It was green velvet with a matching green satin ribbon tied in a perfect bow in the back. I felt very special in that dress and made everyone in my family proud as I played my recital piece taught to me by blind Professor Johnson who taught piano at the University of Cincinnati. Mother and Daddy wanted so much for us to take piano from him.

I remember sitting on the piano bench next to him, his empty sightless eyes blinking open periodically allowing me to peek in and see there was no life in them. He cupped his hands and fingers over mine and would say, "Little hammers, Ann, little hammers" indicating how he wanted me to strike the keys.

Regretfully, I didn't continue with Professor Johnson too long after that first recital. The commute for Daddy to take me to the University down town and my displeasure with practicing and frankly unenamoured with the piano cut my playing days short. Now I could kick myself.

Ginny's Aunt Dottie took the bus to Hamilton to frequently visit her sister Carole at the Boone's. Aunt Dot would always come bearing toys for all of us to play with. Our most time consuming was on the floor playing Jacks.

Mrs. Boone would make lunch of warm tomato soup and "toasties," little bits of toasted bread cut into small squares to dot the top of the soup. Today we call them croutons.

Ginny's dog, Sporty, was and old cocker spaniel that actually belonged to her older brother, Garrett Jr., or "Boonie" who was away at DePauw University. The only sad memory I have of Alberton Avenue was the day Ginny ran over to our house wailing with grief and tears.

"Mrs. Poole, Spowty died." Ginny had difficulty pronouncing her "r's."

Mother took Ginny in her arms and prayed a little prayer for Sporty. She felt better and ran back across the street.

Early recollections of the Millville Church of the Nazarene revolved around Daddy and Mother singing duets for Sunday morning service and going to Sunday School in the church's lower level. It was here that Mrs. Doenges would sit at the piano and play familiar choruses such as, *"Jesus Loves Me"*, *"This Little Light of Mine"* and *"Jesus Wants Me For a Sunbeam"*. It was in these small Sunday School classrooms that we learned the Bible from cover to cover through the stories that little boys and girls could understand.

Mostly we learned how Jesus came to teach us how to love God and to love each other as ourselves. As a young girl those early days in Sunday School, Vacation Bible School and day-by-day in the pastor's home, began to form my childlike faith. Now, like then, I simply believe without hesitation, intellectualizing, or doubt.

My first recollection of being a "preacher's kid" was being expected to memorize a piece for the children's Christmas program. Unlike Tot, it took me until I was three years-old before I was ready to stand in from of the congregation. Compound the lateral lisp with which I spoke, which means my "s's" would come from the sides of my mouth often accompanied with plentiful saliva, I was embarrassed to speak in public.

But dutiful I was. My first speech was a four line ditty that went like this:

> "I never spoke a piece before,
> I hope I see it through;
> I wish a Merry Christmas,
> To you and you and you."

It must have been a hit with the congregation as soon enough I was up front once again, this time singing a solo:

> *"I don't have to wait until I'm grown up to be loving and true;*
> *There are many little deeds of kindness, that each day I can do.*
> *I can read my Bible and pray, be a loving helper always,*
> *I don't have to wait until I'm grown up, to be what Jesus wants me to be."*

Tot and I were often teamed up for a duet, or we would join with Daddy and Mother to sing a "special" in a Sunday service. Tot's musical ear was pitch perfect when it came to harmonizing, I would take the lead with Daddy, Mom would sing Alto. ***"Our Lord is Leading Us"*** was one of our "sugar sticks" we'd rehearse over and over anytime we'd be in the car:

> ***"Our Lord is leading us to Glory oh how wonderful is He,***
> ***Wonderful is He, wonderful is He,***
> ***Leading us to realms of Glory singing as we go, making known the Love that made us free, that made us free forever;***
> ***Wonderful salvation He is offering to all, offering to all, offering to all,***
> ***Wonderful is He who leads us lovingly above,***
> ***Wonderful, Wonderful, Wonderful***
> ***Is He to me."***

One of my most favorite memories of Hamilton was the rush that would happen after church on Sunday morning. We'd pile hurriedly into the car and make our way downtown Hamilton to the stately bank building on the corner across from Robinson-Schwinn, the department store.

On the second floor of the bank building was the studios of WHMO Radio. I can still feel my little chubby legs running up the stairs embedded with small black and white square tiles just in time for the station employee on duty to unlock the door for us. He'd usher us girls into a small room with a window looking into the sound-proof room where Mother was sitting at the piano and Daddy standing at the upright microphone.

It was here that they would open their 15-minute radio harmonizing a short chorus:

> ***"Wonderful, wonderful Jesus, in the heart He implanteth a song,***
> ***A song of deliverance, of courage, of strength;***
> ***In the heart He implanteth a song."***

Daddy would deliver his message, most likely an abbreviated version of the morning's sermon at Millville. A massive red Coca-Cola machine hummed along in the room where we waited. Our station host put four nickels into the machine and one-by-one he'd pull the small Coke bottles out and hand one to Tot, Cathy, Jan and me. Cold. Delicious.

About the time we finished our drinks, the folks would be reprising their song and signing off until next week.

I loved being in the radio studio.

When we moved to Bethel in 1955, I was in the third grade and made quick friends with Marilee Howard and Andrea Hannah. Andrea's dad owned the local hardware store. The boys in our group included Ricky Venable whose family owned the local Handy Store with free delivery service, and Billy Gaskins, whose dad was the local pharmacist and owned the local pharmacy. Both boys were my boyfriends at one time or another.

I recall attending Billy's birthday party that first year I was in Bethel, 8 years old. He had a record player blaring the tunes of the day that were unfamiliar to me because in our home this 'worldly music' were not permitted. No rock and roll for us.

Little did my folks' know that Tot had somehow acquired a transistor radio and would tuck it under her pillow to secretly listen to the popular station WING in Dayton. One of songs on the top of the charts was "At The Hop."

And it was that very song, "At The Hop," that led me to yield to the temptation to DANCE!

Yes, I danced at Billy Gaskins birthday party. And Tot of all people, snitched on me. When we got home she promptly told mother that "Ann danced" and once again I was ushered into the bedroom by mom who invited to me kneel and ask Jesus to forgive me.

I did. He did.

After that day Tot and I made a pact. "I won't tell on you if you won't tell on me." That pact stayed firm for the rest of our sister life. We were each other's vault.

My final four years in Bethel hold memories of family picnic gatherings on the Ohio River, basketball games, church-related friends and activities.

The sweetest memories revolved around the holidays when our folks would take us to Shillito's in Cincinnati to select our new outfits. How they did it, budget for new clothes for us at Christmas and Easter, was an act of discipline and financial planning. The department store 'charge card' was a new concept in shopping and Mother used her Shillito's card wisely. She would charge at Easter and by the time Christmas rolled around, the card would be paid off for the next round of purchasing.

We'd never be dressed alike in the various sizes of one style. The only time I recall we'd receive the same style would be in the pajamas we'd receive for Christmas; Tot's were always red, mine were blue. But for our special holiday dresses, Mother would allow us to choose for ourselves. Early on we began to establish our own sense of style. Tot would choose patterns or plaids, I chose solids with subtle texture. She more eclectic. Me more classic.

We'd return home from our full day of shopping and excitedly rush to our upstairs "dormitory" in the small cottage parsonage to don the new duds. We'd then proceed down the stairs, one-by-one to parade in front of Daddy for his ooohs and ahhhs of approval.

He was so proud of his girls, especially around the holidays. I was thirteen. The call from Dayton Knollwood came. Daddy and Mother made the decision, after much prayer and conversation, to take this call.

7
Following The Call To Beavercreek

The Beavercreek School System had a teaching position open and waiting for Mother in the fifth grade which she loved. Ferguson Junior High School was so new that the floors were still without final tile. I was assigned to a homeroom in that building where all I recall was cinderblock. Mr. Foskuhl was my homeroom teacher and seated me in alphabetical order behind Jerry Plunkett. Jerry and I would share homerooms throughout the rest of our schooling.

The next four years for me at Beavercreek revolved around my friendship with Marcia Morgan. Her parents, Don and Marjory, were of the Morgan's who organized and built the church where Dad now pastored.

They lived in a spacious home on LaGrange Road complete with a swimming pool. They drove Cadillacs and Thunderbirds. Don was a pilot of his own four-seater plane. They owned a 32-foot Cris-Craft boat on Put-In-Bay in Sandusky on Lake Erie.

Marcia wore beautiful clothes. Her closet was filled with shoeboxes all lined up and labeled. She was generous to allow me to borrow a sweater or a pair of shoes. Again, a friend helping me to put a look together for a special event.

The Morgan's took me in as their 'other' daughter. Everywhere they went, they took me, too. If there was a wedding reception in Michigan on a Sunday afternoon, we'd jump in the plane and fly up for the event. If there was a charity event for the unfortunate, Don and his friend Bill Lang, would dress up as clowns and we'd go to be a part of the festivities. The Home Show in Dayton always drew celebrities, among them ventriloquist Jimmy Nelson, his dummy Danny O'Day and puppet dog Farfel. This was the first exposure I had to a real celebrity and the feeling of being star-struck.

During the summer of our Sophomore year, Marcia's granddad and grandmother Morgan invited us to spend the summer in San Diego. Giggling and excited, we packed our bag, and piled into the car with her Uncle Lloyd, Aunt Velma and Cousin Larry. We made the 2,168 mile trip finally arriving at the Grand Morgan's in La Mesa three days later.

Two 16-year old girls and we were California dreamin.' This was right smack in the height of the Beach Boys music, Woodies with surfboards on the beach, and palm trees swaying in the San Diego breezes. A far cry from Dayton, Ohio.

We squeezed lemons from Gran's tree on the back patio, daily rinsed our hair with a concoction making it California girl blonde in the warmth of the sun. We slathered our body in Baby Oil and sat on the chaise lounges out on the patio for hours to get that perfect tan.

Uncle Joe Morgan was the pastor of San Diego First Church of the Nazarene, so naturally we'd attend the services faithfully on Sunday and Wednesday evenings with the elder Morgan's. Another opportunity for spiritual growth was one week during that summer to attend the Southern California District Youth Camp in Lake Arrowhead. We made special pals, Marcia enjoyed the humor of Ernie Berry and I was smitten by Ralph McCall. Both attended the church and were great to take us to the beach, to the drag races, to get a burger.

Speaking of eating burgers, Grandad's favorite tradition place for a Saturday night burger was "KITTY'S." At first glance you'd never want to step foot in the broken down trailer that spewed smoke from the grill out the top stack. Kitty was the master chef and ran the place like a military sergeant. And she could make the most juicy, perfectly-seasoned, bun-falling-apart burger ever. We'd sit at the counter on rickety round stools with their torn vinyl seats and smother our faces in the sight, smell and taste of our weekly treat.

The other dining tradition would come on Sundays after church, we'd make our way to Anthony's Fish Grotto where we'd dine on the specialty fish and chips served up in the old tyme style of newspaper with vinegar on the side. Grandad loved to eat and loved to share his dining experiences. So generous.

He and Gran, Marcia and I began our cross-country trip back to Ohio in their lovely Cadillac. We laugh still about how Grandad would be obsessive about finding a radio station without static as we made our way through the mountains or the plains. It was the era of car radios with buttons that settled on one station at a time. He would push a button, then another and another….until he'd get frustrated and turn the whole thing off.

We'd sit in the backseat and giggle all the way home to our junior year at Beavercreek. Little did I know what that year would bring to our family, our church, and my friendship with the Morgan's.

The highlight of school that year was Marcia and me winning the leading roles in our Junior Class play, *"Don't Take My Penny."* I played Penny's older sister Mavis, Marcia was our mother. My character was a radio voice over actress with aspirations of making it big in New York City.

Class officer elections resulted in my being voted in as secretary. This new focus, along with the responsibility of our class hosting the Junior/Senior Prom, brought so much activity and I needed to get myself around to tend to all the details. I needed to pass my driver's license test the first time 'round, and I did!

The spring quickly came and soon we were into summer and off to St. Mary's for our district Youth Camp, It was here that I began dating Ron Applegate, a fellow preacher's kid from Cincinnati. The fall of my senior year was Ron's freshman year at the University of Cincinnati to study history. Our school activities and studies kept us occupied during the week, and on the weekends Ron would make the 53 mile trip to visit for an evening. His mother, Virginia, waited for him in her rocking chair until she knew that he was home safe and sound.

My interest in Ron, continuing the duties of class secretary and taking "Mavis'" lead on wanting to appear on stage, I expressed an interest in the local Junior Miss Pageant.

This began a firestorm for our family. Thinking that everyone would be excited and pleased that I could actually qualify for and be accepted into the Junior Miss applicants, I was shocked when Mother balked at the idea.

"Mark my words," she said to me. "There will be people in the church who will not be in favor of your participating in this beauty pageant. They will leave." These words and her anxiety created a "crosspull" for me.

"This is NOT a beauty pageant. It's an achievement and scholarship opportunity. No slinky dresses. No revealing bikinis. Talent, personality, scholarship. Why would anyone leave the church over this?"

One night I walked through the living room headed to bed, Daddy stopped me. "I want to tell you something," his soft voice compelled me to sit down across from him. "Just because you're a Christian you don't ever need to take a backseat to anyone."

I sighed. He continued, "If you want to be in this pageant, do it."

Mother was right. There were families who left the church over it. To my folks' credit, they never made any reference to my being the reason. They just loved me and supported me as I proceeded to take my place in the Greene County pageant where I quoted Psalm 121 *"I will lift up my eyes unto the hills from when cometh my help, my help cometh from the Lord who made heaven and earth….."* and then segued into singing *"The Sound of Music."* This was my talent. Along with the other contestants, I was able to make it through the physical fitness section of the voting, and then the final question.

Finally, there we were, all twelve high school senior girls representing Greene County, standing in a row on the stage of Beavercreek High School auditorium. The third and second place runners-up were named. My heart pounded. My spirit drooped thinking, " I didn't even place!"

"And now, ladies and gentlemen, Greene County's Junior Miss for 1965, ANN POOLE!"

The crown, the roses, the other girls coming to congratulate me; my family rushing to the stage, camera flash bulbs bursting all around....it was surreal.

I won! I actually won!

I caught a glimpse of Mother, holding back, tears filled her eyes. Pride and fear gripped her.

We prepared for the Ohio State Junior Miss Pageant scheduled within just a few weeks. Hair appointment, wardrobe planning including formal presentation dresses, accessories including hats and gloves. Each item checked off the to-do list. I was ready to go yet heading into the experience with some trepidation.

The current Greene County Junior Miss went on to win the Ohio Junior Miss title the year before. Connie Lockwood was a role model, as was Pam Robinson who'd made Beavercreek proud two years earlier as Ohio's Junior Miss, then onto Miss Ohio in the Miss America Pageant. I had these two lovely young women to look up to and two consecutive years of winners staring me in the face.

Fortunate, the week's activities were planned in neighboring Xenia, Ohio and although only a few miles from our home, I was required to move into a local host home and share a room with one of the other pageant winners. My roommate was Becky Shriver from Cochoctan. She loved sign language and offered a beautiful passage from "The Miracle Worker," the story of Helen Keller, as her talent. She took the talent trophy. I was so proud.

The Ohio State pageant was well attended by family and friends of the participants from all over Ohio. Friday night we were divided into two groups alternating the talent, physical fitness and interview presentations.

After that first night of competition, Daddy came to me with these words, "I don't think you're going to win, Ann. The girl from Mt. Vernon, Janie Pilotti is very talented and I think she's got it sewn up."

Thud. My heart sank. I knew he was right.

I thought of one last ditch effort I could make to bring a trophy back to Beavercreek. Miss Congeniality! The contestants were gathered backstage before the beginning of the Saturday night competition. Our model trainer, Bette Massie, explained we would now cast our individual vote for Miss Congeniality.

"Simply check the name of the girl from the list who you believe has best integrated with the other girls and represented the best of the Junior Miss qualities on and off stage."

I voted for myself. I received one vote.

Saturday night when I stepped onto the stage, I gave it my best shot. Spoke my scripture, sang my song. Took my bow.

Dad's prediction came true. While we all waited holding our collective breath, the MC made the announcement, "Ladies and Gentleman, Ohio's Junior Miss 1965, from Knox County and Mt. Vernon, Miss Jane Pilotti!" Another chapter in my life, I thought, had come to a close.

With Dad's encouragement, I entered.
With Mom's anxiety, the church folks left.
I won the county's crown.
I lost the title of Miss Congeniality.
I lost the state crown.

Done? Not even. The exposure to this level of glamour and fashion, poise and appearance, hair and accessories intrigued me and would propel me into the world of beauty as my life and times progressed.

Expending so much the time and energy being Greene County's Junior Miss, "the Greene Queen" as my sisters called me, there was little of me left over for my friendships and other school activities.

There was always time for church. Especially now since I felt an extra obligation to be the peacemaker for all those faithful followers who'd stuck with us through the exodus. My friend Marcia went on to star in the Senior Class Play and created new connections. Although still 'besties' it was evident we began to go our separate ways.

Ron and I continued our long-distance relationship and made it through my graduation and the summer of '65. I worked for a local pediatrician, a diminutive but strong Chinese woman, YuRu Yuan. She hired me as her office receptionist. My career interest had now turned to medicine, as in becoming a nurse, and this position gave me opportunities to assist with the various bumps, bruises and breaks that would come with our small patients.

Working had always been a way of life for me. From the fourth grade in the small print shop owned by church members in Bethel, to the catalog department at Montgomery Ward in Xenia, to the front desk in Dr. Yuan's office, and for National Cash Register as a summer temp office helper, I loved earning my own money to be able to tithe to the church, to give unexpected gifts to my family and friends and to afford the things I wanted.

My summer at Dr. Yuan's provided funds to pay for the extras I'd need as I headed to Bethany Nazarene College, in Bethany, Oklahoma to begin my nursing education. BNC was one of six colleges affiliated with the Church of the Nazarene and the only one in the mid-60's with a nursing program. Oklahoma City was a long 16-hour drive from Dayton, and Olivet would have been closer our family history and in distance. I stuck with my decision to go to BNC.

Daddy and Mother once again used creative financing to get me registered in Bethany. We needed a total of $1,500 for tuition, fees, room and board for the first semester. They made a deal with our bank manager and mortgaged their car, a Pontiac. Along with a gift from church members Dick and Louise Ditmer and my Bearinger grandparents, I was able to pay the bill.

Away from home, apart from Ron, I began to feel the freedom they say often happens. BNC was a conservative, private Christian school, and never once was I tempted to break any rules or regulations. I just wanted to be popular, to meet as many people as I could and get involved with as many activities as time would allow.

Early in the semester I caught the attention of an upper class student who lived off campus. He wanted to take me out. I was intrigued. I was interested. Although Ron and I promised to 'stay true' to each other through the separation, I was headed down a path that would break that promise.

I went out on a date with the upperclassman. I called Ron to 'fess up' and told him straight out what I had done. He hung up on me and we never spoke nor saw each other again.

My grades that first semester reflected my life as "social butterfly." The classes required for a nursing degree were more demanding and strenuous than I was willing to discipline myself to study. Quiz after quiz, lab after lab, final after final, I did marginally until one day I was called into the Academic Dean's office.

Dr. Harold Ripper was a kind but firm man. He pulled no punches, didn't waste any time. He wanted me to know he was putting me on the "Dean's List" ~ however not the one you would write home about. The "probationary dean's list" would give me one more chance to focus on my studies and pull my grades up, or else, I'd be heading home to Dayton.

I got serious. And I changed my major. I entered the gym and the process of beginning a major in physical education. Becoming a life guard the same summer I worked for Dr. Yuan, I worked at a community pool in Dayton. This prepared me for a few hours of work as life guard at the college pool located in the physical education facility.

From our experience at home in Bethel with the boys and basketball, I loved being in the gym and was hired as a secretary for the head of the department. I enrolled in my classes, enjoying the theory or practical learning.

It was during a class in Badminton that I felt my right knee dislocate and I knew that my life in this field would be cut short as a participant. And I decided to shift majors yet one more time.

Thankfully the Home Economics department was in the same building facility as the physical education department. Just up the stairway, I found my favorite major professor, Dr. Anne Greve and my home in a major that she helped me craft, the first of its kind, in Fashion Merchandising. Her guidance, and modeling what a single woman could accomplish including building her own log cabin in Colorado, throughout the next two years paved the way for what was to come in for the next forty years in my life and career.

These years also gave lifelong friendships, that I cherish to this day, in Laura (Price) Moore, Margaret (Wallace) Eaton and Linda (Brown) Gresham.

8
Now When The Next One Came Along, They Surely Wanted HIM. But HE Turned Out To Be A Girl, They Called Him Cathy Lynn

"Her name, we're gonna call her, Caffy, Caffy Wynn."

Those were Totty's words when asked about the baby who was on the way. Back in the day, Mother's Dr. Lehman didn't have ultrasound to pre-tell the sex of the baby. So, the natural tendency was to believe that after two daughters perhaps the third would be a son.

There was a member of the Millville Church who had graduated from Harvard and calculated that Wes and Pauline had a 16:1 chance of having a boy after having four daughters. But after two perhaps the chances were greater.

SHE arrived on October 20, 1949 just two years and ten months after "little Ann." Mother called Cathy her "porcelain doll" because her skin was as pure and perfect as the driven snow. She was a tiny baby, too, making her just the size of a baby doll.

Perhaps it was because the anticipation was for a boy, Cathy became Daddy's right hand girl. She loved being outside with him digging in the dirt planting flowers and shrubs. She looked forward to going fishing with Uncle Hermie and Aunt Anna Mae Word. She became a great sports fan and to this day enjoys all things sports, baseball, basketball, football both professional and college.

Cathy's elementary school years were spent in the Bethel school system and almost from the beginning those years were unfriendly, uncomfortable, bordering on painful.

One day in the cafeteria, after eating lunch, she got sick on the milk, perhaps it had soured, and she vomited. Right there in front of all her classmates she then slipped and fell in the vomit. Humiliated. All she heard was laughter. It changed her forever.

She did NOT want to go to school from then on. Mother would have to pay her a dime each morning to prompt her into the car. Cathy would cry. No, Cathy would wail. It was a pitiful thing to watch and hear. My heart went out to her every single day.

Cathy found ways to compensate for the distress facing her each day at school. She began to gain weight due to overeating to fill that place of anguish inside. She began rebellious activities including pulling up dried grass from the yard, rolling it in newspaper and smoking it like a cigarette. She'd spend many hours next door with a kid named Johnny and his grandmother doing who knows what…..

Although a part of our family and bearing the same expectations as a preacher's daughter, Cathy seemed to march to her own drum. In high school she fell in true love with one of the boys in the Knollwood church, Gary Brown, a handsome kid with a beautiful singing voice. He was just a year older than Cathy and was kind to give her attention, but not the kind of attention for which she so longed.

It broke her heart when in a few years, Gary chose another girl to be his wife. He eventually took ill, and died at an early young adult age.

Daddy, Mother, Jan and I had just pulled into Oklahoma City in the fall of 1967 to return me to BNC for the beginning of my junior year. We received a call from one of the church members reporting on a "raucous party going on at the parsonage." Without hesitation, my folks and little sister Jan jumped back in the car and began their 16-hour journey back to face the music with sister Cathy and the church board.

This was now strike three. First Tot with her unplanned pregnancy. Then me with my involvement with the Junior Miss Pageant. Now Cathy and the party in the parsonage. The words that were spoken by Don

Morgan, Marcia's dad, struck my father in the heart and started the motion for him to resign from Knollwood and to accept another pastorate in Middletown.

Those words, "If you can't control the actions of your own daughters, how can you expect to help us raise our own children," began the shift for all of us.

Cathy registered at the Miami Valley Hospital's Licensed Practical Nursing program. She loved the idea of serving through the healing profession. She continued to live at home with the folks in Middletown while commuting to Dayton for her daily coursework. Following graduation Tot and Doug invited her to live with them at Olivet and become "Nanny" to little Heather Dawn.

The relocation was the best thing that ever happened to her, and for her. She was a loving helper to Totty and found employment at the local hospital in Kankakee. It was here that she cared for a patient by the name of Larry Allgood, a transplant to Illinois from Mississippi. Larry thought Cathy was the most beautiful woman in the world and fell in love with her.

When he proposed and told her they would move back to his home place in Starkville, she said "yes," with one caveat. And he agreed. She wanted to be able to come home to Ohio every six months. It didn't happen.

They made it home infrequently. She was working full-time in a facility for the mentally challenged; he was a meat cutter in a local market. They moved into a lovely three bedroom home down a lane, far back in the pines. When Daddy first drove down that lane he said to Mother, "No daughter of mine is going to live out here in the sticks." He soon fell in love with the familiar surroundings, reminding him of "down home."

Since the Allgood's couldn't make it home on a regular basis, Daddy and Mother made an "October birthdays" trip each year to celebrate Larry, Cathy and Daddy's collective birthdays. Larry would take Daddy hunting which he loved. Thick t-bone steaks would have been hand-selected by Larry at the market to treat the folks for the birthday dinner. Larry respected and loved Cathy's folks.

A baby girl, Jenice Christine, was born in 1973, followed by daughter Erin and then son Justin. These three brought Cathy great joy as she loved babies in general, but adored her very own.

The work schedules, Cathy taking the children to church and Larry either working or staying home, compounded by use of alcohol, all began to take their toll on their marriage and little home. The kids would go to school and come home to their grandmother, Larry's mother Christine, who'd watch them until Cathy would return from work.

At one Christmas break, I flew to Starkville to visit and carry gifts to place under their Christmas tree. Jenice was like her mother in having gained weight during her high school years. She was slovenly when I was there. I couldn't understand how a young, bright high school girl could be so lazy.

Within a few days after my visit I received a call from Cathy. During the night Jenice asked her mother to take her to the hospital because her stomach was aching "really bad." When they arrived at the local hospital they took Jenice to the second floor.

Familiar with the layout of the hospital, Cathy said to the admitting nurse, "The second floor? That's the maternity floor!"

"Yes, that's right, Mrs. Allgood. Your daughter is having a baby."

The shock of all shocks. For nine months this child had kept this pregnancy a secret under the guise of her weight. Not even her best friend knew she was expecting.

As by Divine appointment, the delivery doctor happened to have a friend who wanted so much to adopt a newborn. Within moments of the delivery, the agreement was made that this beautiful baby, a girl, would find safe harbor in the home of the doctor's friend. She, like Cheryl, would be the adoptive parents' princess.

One by one, the Allgood children graduated from Starkville High School; Jenice followed in her mother's career footsteps as an LPN; Erin wanted to follow her dream of being an artist, a photographer, and finally a massage therapist, which she did. Justin found his talent and purpose after a brush with the law and finishing his GED. He found a lovely bride in Brandilee and together they established their home in which to raise their two boys, Wesley and Camryn.

Within a few years Jenice once again found herself pregnant, this time with a son who she named Jordan. He was a beautiful child, with a sweet spirit and enduring love for his mother and his grandmother who he called "Mamie."

All the way through elementary and junior high school, Jordan's natural talent for baseball carried him through the Little League World Series in St. Louis where he was named Most Valuable Player by the coaches. He dreamed of playing professional baseball returning someday to St. Louis to play for the Cardinals. He was in a great place to develop his skills with coaches that believed in him. Heading out of high school to Mississippi State he was being followed by scouts.

Then the unfathomable happened, he injured his shoulder and it took him out of the game and out of his dream.

Jenice and her mother were best friends and confidantes. They traveled with Jordan's team to the games and were his biggest fans and cheerleaders. They, too, were devastated at the dash of his big league dream.

Jenice became increasingly distressed in her abdomen and was diagnosed with Crone's disease. For years she was in constant pain, couldn't eat to keep anything down. Was losing weight and strength. She had to quit working. And was constantly in anxiety over her failed attempts to get the state to help her with her medical needs. We wrote letters to Senators and Congressmen.

We enlisted her baby daughter's father who was now a state representative, to help in the cause. Mother, Daddy and I personally stepped in to help with whatever financial support she would need month-by-month.

Her health became desperate. One Saturday she called her mother with fear in her voice, "Mom, my legs are freezing and have gone numb."

Within moments they airlifted Jenice to a hospital in Jackson where the decision to amputate both of her legs below the knees was made to save her from the infection that was rampant through them. Cathy stood vigil at her daughter's side in recovery. As a nurse, she looked at all the medical hook ups, tubes, wires attached to Jenice's body. Her one regret is that she didn't get "close enough" to her thinking that she would disturb some vital functioning of a monitor or machine.

Cathy left Jenice after she spent those few moments with her in recovery. Within just a few moments she was given the shocking news. "Jenice has experienced cardiac arrest."

"She is gone."

Although Cathy had her husband Ronnie, and children Erin and Justin to surround her and Jordan, "a part of me died with her," in Cathy's words.

The evening of Jenice's viewing and the day of the service there were throngs of friends and family who lined up to get into pay their respects. In the deep South, we saw black and white, old and young, white and blue collar. Each one greeted by my sweet sister. For the first time I saw that Cathy had developed her own "mission" in this part of the world, she was "Mamie" to all of them. They loved her and came to tell her so.

The chapel of the lovely funeral home was packed to capacity, standing room only. Cathy walked to the podium and we held our breath.

She began, "I know you are wondering, HOW in the world is the mother of this child able to speak in this moment?"

Cathy paused and looking at Jan and me sitting in the front row, she continued, "I can do this because I'm a Poole and this is what we do." She spoke, she sang. She made it through "because she's a Poole and this is what we do."

We might as well have buried Cathy on the day we laid Jenice to rest in a plot right next to her daddy, Larry Allgood. She was his princess. They were now together in Heaven as Jenice's final words to her mother were, "Don't worry Mom, God's got this."

Larry had made his peace by accepting the Lord in the presence of Daddy on one of their emergency trips to Mississippi in the final days of Larry's dwindling life.

We are confident that it's "all good" with both Larry and Jenice's souls. Yet even with the promise that one day they'll be reunited, Cathy was still dying inside.

Cathy had come through her own bout of breast cancer, had been in remission for a year or two, and wondered now why the Lord spared her and took Jenice. Those kinds of questions and thousands more flooded Cathy in the days and months to come. She chose to stay home, to be reclusive; attending church or the Friday night "singin's" with local musicians dramatically ended. Except for family and her closest friends who came to visit, she had zero interest in anyone, anything, anytime.

The healing continues. With her connections on Facebook we see a sister that has seemed to have "turned the corner" in her grief. Although something that cannot be rushed, her grief is now taking its rightful place and the activities of her life are beginning to wake up again. Singing, playing her bass guitar, shopping, enjoying having family home for Thanksgiving and Christmas……all indications that she realizes Jenice is not coming back and she must go on with her life.

9
Janet Marleah Brought With Her A Love So Pure And Sweet
Pauline's Dream To Have A Girl's Quartet Was Perfectly Complete

It was May, 1952 just eight days before Mother's 32nd birthday, Millville Church was in revival. It was Friday night and Dr. Lehman had suggested that Mother head to the hospital for the birth of baby number four.

Daddy delivered the expectant mother to Ft. Hamilton Hospital, waited with her until the last minute and then announced, "I must get the evangelist and get to church."

With that, he kissed his bride and walked out the door. "Well, Lord, I guess you and I are going to have this baby by ourselves."

And they did.

Janet Marleah, named after Mother's baby sister Jan, arrived healthy, pure and sweet.

Jan was a good baby and so much fun for us to have our own baby doll. Totty was seven-years old when Jan came into our family, was most helpful to Mother watching the baby and she enjoyed being the perfect "little mother."

The nickname, "Janet Marleah Wet-Pants Poole" followed her all the way through her diaper-wearing days. Seemed like she was always needing to be changed.

Early on, Tot and Jan bonded and their relationship would grow stronger through the years, especially when Tot and Heather moved back home to Middletown when Doug bailed the first time.

I don't know what caused her shift from "sweet" to "sour" in her early years.

However, as the baby of the family, she had one dad and four mothers. No wonder she would opt to bang her head on the concrete sidewalk in front of our house when she didn't get her way. No wonder she put her fist through the front door one Sunday afternoon when she decided she'd pose as a magazine salesperson. She gathered her 'products' and headed outdoors.

Within just a few minutes we heard the doorbell ring. Tot went to the door. Opening it she saw a 5-year old Jan standing there and before giving her a chance to make her pitch Tot said, "We don't want any." She slammed the door in Jan's face.

Button pushed! Jan was so mad, she rammed her hand through the storm door, shattering the glass and causing a gash that required stitches from Bethel's local family doctor, Dr. Simmons.

We caught a glimpse of her "other side" and I, for one, determined not to go there if I could help it.

Daddy's schedule enabled him to be our personal "bus driver" which made our daily routine during the school year a family affair. He would drop mother and the three of us girls at our various school and take Jan, not yet school-age, with him as he went about his pastoral duties visiting shut-ins, the hospital, the church. They were good pals.

One by one, the three of us graduated and went on our way to college and life. Jan was still at home with the folks when they moved to Middletown. This is where she would graduate and experience her first racially integrated school. As much as Tot didn't love Beavercreek, that much Jan didn't love Middletown, even though Mother would put a spin on it by saying, "It's the All-American City."

And All-American it was. Middletown's athletics has been put on the map more than once with Jerry Lucas Ohio State and NBA basketball player, Cris Carter Hall of Fame NFL player, Kyle Schwarber Chicago Cubs Major League Baseball Catcher, Jalin Marshall Ohio State Wide Receiver and a member of the first College Football Championship in January 2015.

Additionally, culture and arts were enriched by Middletonians as The Maguire Sisters and Miss America Susan Perkins called Middletown home.

Still, Jan didn't love it.

So, she put her interest and energy into Dad's local church and the Southwestern Ohio District church activities. She inherited her beautiful vocal singing talent from our folks and was selected to be a part of the District Impact Team. Impact was a selected group of exceptional teens who were willing to present the gospel in word and song as they were sent on the weekends to youth programs, during the summer to camps.

One of the members of the Impact group was a young man from Dayton First Church of the Nazarene. His name, Bob Tocheff.

The seemingly perfect match resulted in marriage and three perfect babies within three years. "Sometimes," Jan said, "I'd look at these three children and say 'when are the parents going to come and pick these kids up?'"

Seemingly perfect wasn't so, and the Tocheff's made the choice to divorce. Jan established a second safe harbor for Kyle, Kim, Clay and their friends. Keeping them in church, helping them with school projects, supporting them in their sports and hobbies kept the vital connection they needed growing up.

Jan completed her master's degree in education and in the high school world in which she lived, she was recognized as Teacher of the Year by the students three separate times, she hosted the annual Veterans Day recognition program always bringing the crowd to tears. Her devotion to our heritage, Jan has become the archivist of our family. She keeps the traditions and it is her home with her husband, Don Quinn, where we all head when we need that touch, taste, sounds and scent of "home."

Yes, there were four of us preacher's daughters lovingly referred to as the "four little puddles." When Daddy would be asked about all girls and no boys, he would smile and say, "I got my girls at the hospital, I'll get my boys at the altar."

And so he did. Among the four of us, there were six divorces and nine trips to the altar. We gave him more than his share of boys.

Around our home we celebrated the memory-making events of most families, although I believe we celebrated more than most. Whatever was happening in the lives of our immediate group (graduations, weddings, anniversaries, births, promotions, birthdays) and of the those who celebrated in our church and community family, we were there to plan, execute and celebrate.

Our home was the epicenter of these celebrations including our Thanksgiving table laden with the traditional fare, and always the five kernels of corn on each china plate to remind us of our forefathers Pilgrim story of near starvation and their meager beginnings during the formative stages of our country's history, before we began eating our abundant meal.

Mom's Five Kernels of Corn story came from the Society of Mayflower Descendants, claiming during their starving time of 1623, the Pilgrims were down to eating just 5 kernels of corn each day.

The Society claims that the five kernels now represent five legacies of the Pilgrims: the right to stand for one's principles; freedom of religion; majority rule (from the Mayflower Compact's rule by "the consent of the governed"); private enterprise (disbanded communal living to private plots); and an everlasting faith in God.

Always the teacher, beginning in 1995 and carrying on to this day, Tot had us write the word, "T-H-A-N-K-S", in a vertical acrostic on a piece of paper. From the letters' prompts, we each would write what we were most grateful for during the current year.

You can imagine the groans and aggravation at first. As Jan's youngest, a teen, Clay infamously asked, "Why can't we be like others families and just eat turkey and watch football?" Over the 20 years, what a rich collection of our family's history; of what was going on in the lives of each person each year; of our triumphs and tragedies, of funny entries like Sam's "**Tom HANKS**" or Don's list of foods. We also witnessed creative prose.

Even a more mature Clay as a college student wrote his "THANKS" in Spanish! Everyone was put to shame when granddaughter Madelyn, at age five, arrived with her "THANKS" list and a drawing of her family. Now some of us work on our "THANKS" weeks ahead so as not to be brain dead after eating turkey. Mom and Dad usually chose to list their favorite hymns or scripture verses, not a surprise.

Most of all, we are implored to "get still and get grateful" on Thanksgiving Day! Thanks, Tot!

There was Christmas with Daddy dressing up as Santa in the suit that was worn and too small, cotton balls stuck to his face with scotch tape...the little kids could never tell the difference. They were always so happy to see Santa in the flesh calling out their names taped to the packages so lovingly placed under the tree the night before by a devoted Grampa and Gram.

As the folks became less interested and less capable of navigating the mall crowds to do their shopping, Mother would send a Christmas check to each family selflessly written out of her school bonus or Daddy's gift from the church. We would receive it prior to our gathering with the following written instruction: "Please get what you want and wrap it so we can put it under the tree; you can unwrap it and I can see what you chose."

Dutifully, each year, we all did just as she directed. We'd laugh until our sides hurt when acting surprised at the treasures she and Daddy had given us.

These and a host of memories were lodged in the comfortable couch that welcomed a formal pastoral discussion as well as a slouching "I'm home" snuggle; the dining room table that held the precious moments of song and prayer before our meals; the kitchen table and chairs where Mom and Dad would begin their day in the Bible and pray for each of us by name. There was her piano. His Grandfather clock with that perfect Westminster chime gong-gong-gong on the hour all through the day AND the night.

As was our custom I phoned my folks every night at 10:20 and it was no different in 2005 on Monday night, April 4th, as the NCAA Final game between North Carolina and Illinois was wrapping up March Madness.

Just the day before, Jan and Don made the two-hour drive south to Middletown for a visit with the folks. Jan clearly recalls returning to their home following church and lunch at the Grande Dame Manchester Hotel for a visit. Daddy walked through the house and the door into the garage, singing at the top of his lungs:

"Not what I wish to be, nor where I wish to go, for who am I that I should choose my way; The Lord will choose for me, 'tis better far I know, So let Him bid me go, or stay."

Then came the Monday night call. After Mother and I got caught up on the family news, she passed the phone to Daddy and I heard his normal greeting, "Where in the world are you?" That night I was in my "pod" apartment mid-town, eastside New York City watching the game and enjoying my second bag of microwave popcorn.

While we spoke, Illinois came from a 20-point deficit to tighten up the game. As loyal Ohio State Buckeyes, we're also loyal to the Big 10 and thus were rooting for Illinois all the way.

At one point, he abruptly asked if I was "talking on my cell phone and perhaps we should hang up now." So I told him I loved him, said goodnight and "I'll talk to you tomorrow."

Tuesday, April 5th, I was awakened by my phone ringing, unusual at 7:00 a.m. "Annie," I heard the voice of my brother-in-law Sam Ashworth. "Annie, your dad is gone."

"Gone? Where did he go? How could he be gone? I just spoke to him last night. We were cheering for Illinois!"

"He's gone."

Sam and I made plans for my flight, the first available one to Cincinnati that afternoon. He'd be at the baggage claim when I arrived to take me to Middletown and the beginning of several days of daze as we celebrated, memorialized and buried our dad.

Arriving in Cincinnati, I made the long walk from the terminal to where Sam was waiting. I stepped on the escalator, one of those escalators that's so high it appears that it's a moving stairway to Heaven. As I got closer to the top, I pictured Dad standing there.

He would always be happy to pick me up at the airport, to be the first to welcome me home. This was our time. The 50-minute drive was reserved for our conversations about the church, my work and travels, the family.

He was always dressed in his "working clothes" a suit and tie. In the winter, he'd look so dapper in his black overcoat, classic black hat and leather gloves. Standing at the top of the escalator he'd be wearing another accessory, a name sign emblazoned with "MINCEY" or "REDKEN" just like those presented by professional chauffeurs as they await their passengers.

We'd always laugh. I'd feel his welcoming hug, retrieve my bags and make our way to the car. His car. Mother never drove and even she would refer to the car as "Daddy's car." Often, after he died, she would retreat to the garage and sit in his car just to feel close to him.

This day, though I prayed this was all a mistake and he'd be standing there like always. Daddy wasn't there with the sign. BUT! There was a driver waiting for a passenger and he was holding a sign.

Evidently, the Sunny Delight fruit juice company was in Cincinnati and a driver was holding a sign that simply read, "SUNNY DELIGHT."

Immediately I smiled, "Oh Dad, you're describing Heaven to me!" From that moment on I never had a moment of sadness. I knew he was safe at "home," that he had heard those words we all long to hear from the Lord, "Well done thou good and faithful servant," and he was already out and about enjoying the unfathomable sights and sounds of a land he had preached about his entire life.

The story of how his death happened was told to me by my mother. After we hung up from our call on that April 4th night, mother went to bed which was her custom. She'd always say, "My curtains come down at 11:13 p.m." And they did. She would kiss Daddy good night and head to their bedroom just across the hall from the TV room.

He normally would finish watching the game and as was his custom, he'd stay up to watch the 11:00 p.m. news followed by <u>Nightline</u> hosted by Ted Koppel. But that night, THAT night, he turned off the television and followed mom to the bedroom and to their bed.

"Ann," she said with a glisten in her eye, "our room was turned into a honeymoon suite!"

Pretty wonderful for a couple at 84, and approaching their 62nd year of marriage!

Around 2:00 a.m. he awoke with pains in his chest. She got up with him, assisted as he took the nitroglycerine tabs. The pains were relieved immediately. They returned to bed this time falling into satisfying sleep.

At around 6:00 a.m. mom heard Daddy snoring and reached out to shake him gently, "Wes, turn over, you're snoring." When she touched him he didn't stir. She knew was gone.

In relating the details of this story to me, of course there was sorrow. However, when I saw my father's body at peace in his casket, I did notice he had a smile on his face. Literally.

Mother continued to live alone in our home. More than once I asked her if she "gets scared, or lonely." She'd look at me surprised, "Why should I be scared or lonely? The Lord's here."

Just as real was her relationship with the Lord, as palpable as having Daddy there in the flesh, she literally felt His presence every moment of every day. She lived every day cherishing and caring for their possessions in this "little piece of Heaven."

The little piece of Heaven was their first real home, not a parsonage provided by the church. When they retired they had no home. Nowhere to go. They had invested all they had in making sure that the four of us received our education. Delayed gratification that was never repaid.

Never could mother see herself in an apartment, although she agreed to visit some apartment complexes. None of us wanted that for them.

On an urge from the Holy Spirit, she felt compelled to call a local real estate developer who was also a fellow Christian and friend, Courtney Duff. When Mother explained their current situation, retired with no place to go, Courtney immediately responded with the solution.

"I have a just built a new 3 bedroom home that I would be happy for you and Rev. Poole to live in. I'll make it available to you at my cost." That was the deal. This was the house meant for them. We organized a way that I could participate by investing in their home that gave me a tax deduction and gave them a place to live for the next twenty-two years.

Mom and I continued our ritual of calling every night ending our conversation with a prayer. She wasn't a fan of the eleven-o'clock news. Instead she would fill her heart and mind with devotional readings, watch classic Billy Graham telecasts, or pray for her family. She'd finally relent when her "curtain" would come down at 11:13 p.m. and off to bed she would go...to the double bed where the two of them slept and snored 'in harmony' for sixty-two years.

On a Wednesday in November 2007, two-years and seven months after Daddy went to Heaven, Mother's Senior Citizen City Van 'chauffeured' her to the local Dillard's Salon for her weekly shampoo and set appointment. The highlight of her week was to have her head massaged, sit under the warm dryer, take a nap and then feel refreshed for another seven days.

She wouldn't miss it! She loved Dottie, her stylist, and all the salon professionals, as well as all the other customers who frequented the salon at the same time each week. Every six months it was perm time and today was the day! A fresh perm meant that she wouldn't have to exert as much effort to keep her 'do in place with nightly pin curling, using Velcro rollers and toilet paper wrapped around her head holding her hairstyle in place as she slept.

She sat in Dottie's chair and was remembering Daddy. "Oh Dottie, I miss Wes so much," she said. Those were some of the final words Dottie heard her speak.

Around midnight, Mother was startled by a sharp pain over her left shoulder. It was severe enough that, for the first and only time, she pushed the button on her Lifeline and immediately the EMS team showed up, entered the garage and found her in her bedroom. Administering immediate actions to stabilize her, they then took her to the Middletown Hospital where she was admitted into the ER.

On a gurney for several hours, she was evaluated and the decision was made to admit and monitor her for the day. My sister Jan and her husband Don drove the two-plus hours from Mt. Vernon, my brother-on-law Sam was there when they arrived.

Once she was settled in her room, sitting up and feeling stronger, she asked Don and Sam if they'd return to the house to get a few personal items; a hairbrush, her toothbrush AND her teeth that were in the cup on the bathroom sink.

They boys left to make the one-mile trip to 227 Heatherway. Jan was there with mom and for the next few hours they shared, sang, read scriptures. Mother said the word that came to her that morning was from Exodus 15:2 **"The Lord is my strength and song, and he is become my salvation. I will prepare him an habitation: my father's God and I will exalt him."**

They ordered lunch and were awaiting its delivery when suddenly Mother grabbed her left shoulder, "Oh! There's that pain again!"

As Jan ran toward the sliding glass door to notify the nurse, she reminded Mom of the scripture, Isaiah 26:3 **"Thou will keep him in perfect peace whose mind is stayed on thee."** She looked back and mother was mouthing the words. Those were the last words that her mouth formed. She was gone before Jan could return with the medical staff.

A Code Blue was called for throughout the hospital. Doctors and nurses came to her to aid to give her a fighting change, intubating her with oxygen pumped into her lungs through a ventilator. For several minutes they administered CPR.

At one point, the attending physician asked Jan what she wanted them to do….continue to help mother survive or let her go. Jan asked one simple question, "If she survives is this how she will live, in this comatose state?" The doctor answered affirmatively. Jan simply said, "Let her go. It's her desire, let her go."

All the medical equipment was unplugged, turned off, and mother lie motionless in that room. Her lunch untouched. She was in Heaven.

I was traveling in Australia. My phone rang early in the morning, it was our family friend Joan Etter who, through tears, uttered the unfathomable words, "I hate to have to give you this news, but your mother died this afternoon."

"WHAT? I just spoke to her, it can't be!" Joan was crying. I was a mess. How in the world was I going to explain to the REDKEN team who had invested in my trip all the way from New York City to Australia that I needed to get the first flight from Sydney to LA and then to Cincinnati and miss the very conference for which they had brought me to Australia.

My friends, life-long Aussie friends came to my grieving rescue. First Jim Hogan, a man I shared a committed relationship with, had moved back to Sydney. We made a phone connection and he immediately gathered his family, Tom, Margaret, Kevin to meet us for lunch where I felt their loving care and compassion. Then my friend Dorothy Marlow came from Noosa Heads, the Great Barrier Reef, and we were together when I needed to head to the airport to meet my flight carrying me home to my now deceased mother.

I had just enough time to take advantage of a pass to climb the Sydney Harbor Bridge, a tourist attraction, and I did it! Tethered to the protective guard posts all the way, we made our climb to the high arch of the Bridge and were photographed. I have that photo framed on my desk to remind me of the day Mother made her Heavenly flight and I got as close to her as I could by being on the top of the Harbor Bridge. A layover in Los Angeles allowed for one more friend to meet and sit with me as I awaited my flight to Cincinnati.

Hayward Sawyer, a former college classmate from then, Bethany Nazarene College (now Southern Nazarene University) received the news that my mother had passed. Hayward called me, rerouted and promised to be at the arrivals area at LAX when I landed.

He was. He took me to lunch, listened to my story, offered me his handkerchief to wipe my tears. When I offered to return the hankie to him, he insisted I take it with me, "You may need it."

Finally, after 24 hours in flight, I arrived at the Cincinnati airport, Jan and Don were waiting for me. My luggage didn't make it so Jan let me borrow clothes for mother's memorial the next day. A new black and white knit sweater with pockets and black slacks is what I chose to wear to the visitation. To this very day, Hayward's hankie is in that sweater pocket where it will remain until Jesus returns!

We talked non-stop from the time we got in the car, until we reached the funeral home. Mother was there, dressed like a Queen in her very most beautiful 60th Wedding Anniversary suit dress. Light aqua blue, it matched her eyes which were now closed forever.

Her new perm was coiffed to perfection by Dottie and Sally (one of Mother's hairdressers for years). Her only accessories were a gold calla lily brooch pinned to the left side of her jacket and her wedding ring. There was only one request I can ever recall her making, "When I die, I want to be buried with my ring on and my teeth in!"

And so she was.

She was exactly where she wanted to be. With Jesus, Daddy, my sister Tot, her parents, in-laws, and a host of family and eternal friends, the cloud of witnesses. She, too, had heard the Lord speak those words, "Well done Pauline, good and faithful servant." She was finally home. Her memorial service focused on her favorite song of that title. **"Finally Home"** sung by Kyle so beautifully, sounding like a Heavenly angel.

> *"Just think of stepping on shore and finding it Heaven*
> *Of touching a hand and finding it God's*
> *Of breathing the air and finding it Celestial*
> *Of waking up in glory, and finding it Home."*

It was nearly impossible to fathom a life without both Daddy and Mother. Now it was our responsibility to care for those things she loved, they loved, so dearly.

The major decision was whether to maintain or to sell their home. In a mid-western steel town where there had been For Sale signs on the front lawns of homes for two or more years, who would we find to buy this 'little piece of Heaven?" Did we want to be landlords and rent it? Did we want to maintain it only to visit a few times each year, leaving it without love and life for weeks on end?

On a February afternoon, we received a call from the next door neighbor, Debbie Garrett. Her voice mail was sweet and simple. "If you decide eventually to sell your parents' home, our daughter Becky has just been approved for her first home loan and she would love to buy it."

The little girl who had played on the empty lot next to her parents' home and was upset that a new house was going to be built on her playground, was the same little girl who had followed in Mother's footsteps of being a school teacher and was now sitting across from us in the real estate office taking ownership of that house.

I handed her the front door key with a big ribbon attached, a bouquet of flowers and a stack of her first grade papers with her name perfectly printed on them BECKY GARRETT that we found while cleaning out Mother's dresser drawer.

We hugged, we cried. The bank's closing officer just sat there and shook his head. "I've been doing closings for over thirty years and I've never witnessed a closing like this one."

Now we began the difficult process of purging. What would we do with it all? Every closet, every drawer contained their presence in a written word, a program from an event we attended, a photo memory. Daddy's theological library, Mother's school supplies. What would be discarded to the dumpster, donated to family, church and Salvation Army, and what would we retain as 'essence?"

Jan was in Centerburg, Ohio on February 24th while I was on an airplane headed for Milwaukee. She had just said to her husband Don, "I need an essence room. Somewhere to house some of the folks' things so I don't lose touch of them and our heritage." That day they made their way to the Columbus Home Show where they began exploring the possibility of expanding their home in some way to accommodate the most vital pieces.

The plane ride to Milwaukee that day allowed me to get still and ask myself the vital questions about the stress that this house situation was presenting me, what my reactions had been - mostly sadness thinking that we'd have to disperse our memory - holding treasures. I also asked myself what a more responsive heart answer could be. That answer came in the form of a crude drawing in the form of a box indicating a room extended onto Jan and Don's house.

My 'box' would replicate our family living and dining room. There would be a bedroom, a small bathroom and a galley kitchen. Selfishly I was designing a place where I could go 'home' when I took a break from my REDKEN travels. A new home that would be familiar of our parents' place.

When I called Jan on the following Tuesday, we confessed our ideas to each other, ideas conceived at precisely at the same time, hundreds of miles away from each other. We knew this was divinely inspired and one that we had to act on. And so we did.

Jan's wonderful husband, Don Quinn, is a genius. We've come to label him as the 'guy that fixes broke stuff.' He can do anything. He built his beautiful home on acreage that was once a corn field on the outskirts of Centerburg, a town that Ohio claims is the heart, the geographic center of the state, thus the name. The property includes a pond he excavated stocked with fish for summertime activities for grandchildren to enjoy.

There is a row of trees that surround and reflect the beauty of the changing seasons.

When Jan and I proposed the idea of expansion, investing the small inheritance left by our parents' trust, Don went to work with his nephew to draw up the design. They planned to first dig a five-foot crawl space under the room, smash through the walls of the existing kitchen and one bedroom giving us a newly designed space for entertaining. The bedroom and bathroom were included in the overall plan and also a spacious walk in closet.

On Easter Sunday afternoon, Jan and I donned construction boots, hard hats, and grabbed a shovels for our unofficial groundbreaking ceremony. We were about to embark on the construction of our "Essence Room" a place where the sights, scents and sounds of home could continue to be experienced.

It was spring 2008 in Ohio. No one was building. The housing crises had hit and the construction workers were plentiful. Don's friends came when he called and showed up for work every day; skilled, professional and on time. Home Depot and Lowe's wanted to sell stuff....tile, carpet, sheet rock, decking....it all came with the price that we could afford and were willing to pay.

By April, the "Essence" had taken shape. I stood in the cool of that spring day arm in arm with my dear brother-in-law, and looked through the framed-in patio doors out to the pond now thawed by the sun's rays. "Many people are sad having to downsize and some even leave their homes. Why are we so blessed to be able to actually experience reproduction and expansion?"

The only answer was reflective of our parents' lives of generosity and this was another example of how God was blessing the gifts that had been given over all the years.

Jan and I stood in the driveway of 227 Heatherway as the garage door closed for the final time. The movers were scheduled to arrive in a few days to carry the treasures we'd decided to keep as they still brought us joy. As the door descended we sang the "Doxology" and "Always."

We knew we were doing the right thing to protect and preserve our heritage in this unique way.

I felt much like the Presidents must feel when they replicate the Oval Office at their Presidential Libraries. Every piece of furniture and memorabilia that was meaningful and held particular charm was restored in its rightful place by Father's Day in June, right down to the doilies under the lamps in the living room, the chenille bedspread on the folks' double bed, and the clock once again chiming its familiar Westminster chimes.

The first visit I made after it was completed was an exceptionally emotional one. I entered through the front door, took one look at our living room and flung myself on that couch that was holding out its imaginary arms and saying "Welcome Home, Annie."

I could smell my mother, the combination aromas of Estee Lauder Youth Dew and Downey Fabric Softener. I could hear Daddy singing and the rustling of his newspaper as he turned the pages.

I was home. And this is exactly as we envisioned it would be for us, for our children and grandchildren. To have the 'essence' of our parents living through the memory-holding pieces of home.

As many of you reading this story have experienced, living through a remodeling or construction project is a grueling and challenging time. My forever love and respect go to Jan and Don for having the courage to endure the dust, disorder and the disruption of their 'tranquility base' while the 'essence' was taking shape.

Their faith in the vision is the reason we have our 'little piece of Heaven' our substance of things hoped for, our evidence of things not seen.

And through it all, the message of the song we would sing as the dream quartet: **SURELY GOODNESS AND MERCY SHALL FOLLOW ME ALL THE DAYS OF MY LIFE** as this preacher and his wife firmly stood on the promise.

A pilgrim was I and a wandering
In the cold night of sin I did roam
But Jesus the kind shepherd found me
And now I am on my way home.

Surely goodness and mercy shall follow me
All the days, all the days of my life
Surely goodness and mercy shall follow me
All the days, all the days of my life.

He restoreth my soul when I'm weary
He giveth me strength day by day
He leads me beside the still waters
And guides me each step of the way.

By the pastures green and waters still
He leadeth me, oh yes, He leads He leadeth me
Through the valley dark and shadows deep
He leadeth me, oh yes, He leads He leadeth me.
All the days, all the days of my life.

10
RADIATE
You Are A Star Right Where You Are
The REDKEN Years

My life with REDKEN began as a job - and turned into my life's work, my calling, my mission.

I've found there's a big difference between having a job and having work, meaningful work, purposeful work.

It was 1972, following my divorce from my college sweetheart, Bill Mincey, I took my preacher Daddy at his word when he said to me and my three sisters, "If the bottom ever drops out, you can always come home." I took him up on his promise and moved back to Middletown, Ohio to live with him and Mom.

I had been peddling a new concept in fingernail extension, acrylic powder and liquid used by dentists in constructing tooth replacements. This product line was packaged in a small square box, filled with nail extension forms, liquid and powder. It was my job to introduce the product and demonstrate to professional manicurists the art of nail making.

A former high school classmate had opened a new salon in Dayton and I made a cold call on their resident manicurist. Before I knew it, I was invited to be the receptionist in her new salon. I'd begin working a couple of days a week until I could decide what I would do with my life.

Those two days a week became five. The weeks passed quickly and soon I celebrated a year working with this creative group of stylists and our faithful clients.

I loved the atmosphere of the salon, the sounds, scents, and social climate. It was a great experience to watch women routinely check in with me carrying the weight of the world on their shoulders reflected in their look. Within a matter of moments I witness them leaving with a fresh attitude created by the professional touch and listening ear of their stylists.

The idea of my making a career in the salon business must have come from a deep, unconscious thought perhaps from my childhood.
The sights, sounds, scents of a beauty salon weren't new to me. From the time I was three years old and my best girlfriend and six-year-old neighbor, Ginny Boone, told me to ask my mom if she could cut my hair.

I recall running across the street to our house, opening the front screen door, turning around immediately and returning to Ginny's house to tell her, "Mommy said yes."

Now returning to our home with my newly crafted bangs and hearing the screen door slam behind me I had a much different feeling inside my stomach. I knew I had told a lie, my first untruth of my life. Mother took one look at me, picked me up in her arms and walked briskly to the nearest barbershop.

A red white and blue barber pole was doing its twirling action outside as I was abruptly seated on the wooden slab placed across the armrests of the barber chair. I don't recall crying or feeling scared. We were doing what needed to be done to get the disaster of my crooked bangs straightened out.

There wasn't much to work with, but he did his best.

From then on throughout our childhood, the salon was a place where my parents invested in each of us for regular haircuts and permanent waves. It was important that we were always presentable "as unto the Lord" and our hair was the crowning glory. I can still hear Daddy say, "Ann, comb your hair."

Betty Pride was the local hairdresser in Hamersville, Ohio within few miles of our town Bethel, population 2,500. It was very much like the small village in Thornton Wilder's famous play, <u>Our Town</u>. Dad, a wonderful pastor and mother a popular high school English teacher, our church was on the fast track of growth with people of all walks of life, and especially the high school kids - including the entire Varsity basketball team.

Betty served each of us well, especially around the holidays of Christmas and Easter. They were the most highly populated church-going days of the year and we always got new hair and new clothes to celebrate.

I loved going to Betty's little salon, one room with two styling vanities, a big Coke machine and hood dryers. I can still recall the smell of perms and hairspray, feel the knitted pink or blue roller cap she'd place over the perm rods to keep them in place, and her little drawer where she kept her day's intake of cash.

As Betty was attending to my sisters' hair, I'd pretend that I was at the "front desk" taking care of the salon while Betty took care of the customers. I was 8 years old. A foretaste of my life at Designers' Loft.

Back to Designers' Loft, there was eventually one person who saw my potential on a grander scale. He visited our salon weekly to keep us updated on new products and education. He was our distributor sales consultant, Bob Richman, the owner of Hairdressers' Supply.

Bob walked into the salon one day, took a look at me and said, "There's a job at REDKEN you'd be perfect for." He saw something in me and took a risk to recommend me for a field sales position. Bob made a call to REDKEN's regional manager Bill Gray, and after two positive interviews, I was hired.

On April 1, 1975, I packed my wardrobe into my '73 Olds Cutlass, hitched on a U-Haul trailer filled with my earthly possessions, and drove away from my parent's home. Stopping in Kansas City on the way out to California, I dropped the trailer with a friend to care for my belongings as I made my way to my new life with REDKEN.

I began my career in a new division dedicated to selling nutritional products - vitamins, minerals, protein powder - especially formulated to develop healthy hair, skin and nails from within. Great idea.... ahead of its time. Think about it, in 1975 Joe Weider and Jack LaLanne were the two major forces in health and fitness.

Having graduated from college with a degree in Home Economics with some emphasis on nutrition, coupled with the in-depth training I received from REDKEN, I began to feel comfortable to begin calling on distributors what would supply names of salons to call on and set appointments for in-salon nutrition classes.

One such appointment came as a result of a group gathering that the consultants of Victory Beauty Supply organized. Victory was headquartered in Chicago, this was a small 2-chair barber salon in Highland, Indiana, just over the state border. The barber, Bill Richardson and his wife Pat, were most interested in the 'inner beauty' message of NUTRALON, but as I found during our appointment, they were more interested in the inner beauty of my soul.

We made the appointment date and time, I arrived on Vince Lombardi time ten minutes early. Rather than meeting in their barber shop, I was invited into their home that was connected to the salon through a doorway that led directly to their kitchen.

Suddenly we were sitting at their round table and enjoying a corned beef and cabbage luncheon Pat had prepared. While we ate I presented my nutritional pitch and the products for their consideration.

By the time we finished lunch, I'd finished my presentation and closed the deal with Bill committing to taking our opening order. I was elated, thanked them for the business, for lunch and for their support of REDKEN.

Beginning to pack my selling materials away, I felt Bill's hand on my arm and he spoke.

"Before you go, I'd like to ask you a question." "Sure. Anything," was my response.

"Ann, have you ever accepted Christ as your savior?" He was looking directly into my eyes.

"Oh Bill, I grew up in the church, Sunday School, Vacation Bible School, Revivals, Youth Camp, Christian College, you name it. I've had a rich background with the Lord."

He waited until I took a breath and then asked again, "I didn't ask what your background was, I asked if you've ever invited Christ into your heart as your personal savior." I was stunned. I quickly reviewed all the opportunities across my lifespan, now 28 years, to surrender my heart to Christ. As a child going to the altar when we sang "Into my heart, into my heart, come into my heart Lord Jesus…." Or at youth camp when I felt a tug to offer my life as a missionary to South Africa, but no, I'd have to say "no" I had never intentionally asked Christ into my heart.

That's exactly how I responded to him. "No, Bill, I don't believe I ever have."

"Would you like to? Right now? Pat and I would love to pray with you." I agreed. Bill began to pray a beautiful prayer of gratitude and offered a moment for me to make Christ the Lord of my life. He gave me the words to say. It was priceless.

There was a feeling of joy and lightness. Thanking them and hugging them, I knew they had done exactly what the Holy Spirit had guided them to do. I realized their barber salon was the "front" for their more important mission and that was to model Christ's love and invite others to accept it.

"How amazing," I thought as I drove away, "my whole life I've been exposed to God's love and loving service." I could see how all of it prepared me for that moment of invitation around a kitchen table by the faithful barber stylists leading me to my decision.

After leaving the encounter of a Christ-kind, I found myself literally living on the road, driving from one end of the country to the other encouraging hairstylists to sell the benefits of healthy hair, skin and nails to their clients with concepts they knew little about. That was my job.

To teach them nutrition.

The hours on the road seemed to speed by as I made my way westward, stopping at an occasional roadside restaurant for a snack and a motel to rest my road-weary body.

All along my journey, I'd hand carried a plaque that had hung on the kitchen wall of my grandparents' modest home. The original string my Grandma tied onto the hooks embedded in the back for hanging were still there.

I traveled mile after mile with the plaque on my dashboard and nightly carried it into my motel room as my protector until the morning light would appear. The raised letters spoke truth, reminding me ***"I can do all things through Christ which strengtheneth me."*** Philippians 4:13.

Out somewhere in Arizona, I knew my journey was nearing its completion and in a few hours I'd be entering Los Angeles; my new life, new company, new adventure. My fears began to surface now, and as they mounted I knew of one sure action to take. Call home!

I pulled into the next rest stop, stretched my legs, made my way to a pay phone, and dialed collect. Faithful as always, my beautiful mother answered, "Good morning!" and I burst into tears.

"Mommy, I'm so scared, I don't know if I can do this. I don't know what to expect. It's bigger than I am; I just so scared."

In her quiet, reassuring way, she began to speak, "Honeygirl, just get back in your car and keep driving. In thirty days you won't remember you even went through the desert."

I thanked her for being there, for sharing her wisdom. I got a Pepsi out of the machine and started back to my car. Sitting silently behind the wheel, I put the key into the ignition and the gearshift into drive. My eyes glanced at the plaque that had accompanied me for nearly 2,500 miles. It read, ***"I can do all things through Christ which strengtheneth me."*** "I can do all things," I thought.

"Wait a minute! I can do all things….does that mean I can do anything?"

The answer was a Divine "of course!" I found myself driving with one hand, and with the other exploring the glove compartment for a pencil, pen, paper, napkin...anything to write on which I could capture what would be the first of several poems to be written through me.

I CAN DO ANYTHING

I CAN BE A LIGHT THAT SHINES
I CAN HELP IN EVERY WAY
TO OPEN EYES OF THE BLIND
LISTENING TO THEIR PROBLEMS
WILL HEAL THE WOUNDS OF TIME
LOVING ALL ABOUT THEM
WILL SEE FREE THEIR MINDS

HE WILL GIVE STRENGTH EACH DAY
MY FAITH WON'T HAVE ANY BOUND
I CAN DO ANYTHING
WHEN I LIVE ON HIGHER GROUND
A HIGHER PLANE THAN I HAVE FOUND
EVERYTHING'S ON HIGHER GROUND

I CAN HAVE ANYTHING
SUCCESS WILL COME THROUGH LOVE AND HEALTH
IT WILL BE FOR ALL TO SHARE
IF NOT TO GIVE
WHAT GOOD IS WEALTH
WATCHING LIVES MAKE CHANGES
BECAUSE OF WORDS WE'VE SPOKEN
HOPEFUL REARRANGES
FOR HEARTS THAT ONCE WERE BROKEN

WHAT I HAVE
I WANT TO SHARE
YOU'LL NEVER KNOW WANT OR NEED
I CAN HAVE ANYTHING
WITH FAITH AS BIG AS ONE SMALL SEED

I CAN DO
YOU CAN TOO
ANYTHING
WE'LL HAVE EVERYTHING
WITH FAITH AS BIG AS ONE SMALL SEED

ANN MINCEY
I CAN DO ANYTHING
SLOW BALLAD
INTRO
I CAN DO ANY THING I CAN BE A STAR THAT SHINES
I CAN HELP IN EVERY WAY TO OPEN EYES OF THE BLIND
HE WILL GIVE STRENGTH EACH DAY
HAVE ANY DOUBT
I CAN DO ANY THING WHEN I LIVE ON HIGHER GROUND
D.S. AL CODA
© 1992
WORDS AND MUSIC BY ANN MINCEY
MUSIC PREPARATION BILL STEVENSON

It was December 1975 and I was invited to present to my colleagues at the annual REDKEN national sales meeting. As a newly hired field representative (just eight months at that time) it was my job to train and sell NUTRALON, the nutritional supplement line we had introduced earlier that year.

Unbeknownst to me while on stage, Paula was standing in the back of the room and whispered to one of our employees, Michael Sweeney, "Who is that?" Although Michael and I hadn't met formally, he knew my name and repeated it to Paula.

The next day I was given a summons to meet in her office located in Canoga Park, California. The location of our sales meeting was the Sheraton Universal which meant my driving in a borrowed car north on the frenzied Ventura Freeway 101.

The brisk January air wasn't enough to keep my palms from sweating as I took the DeSoto Avenue exit and found my way, sans GPS, to Variel Avenue and the headquarters of REDKEN Laboratories.

Greeting me in the beautifully appointed lobby was former child star, Gloria Jean. She had been Paula's idol as a young girl and when the time came for Gloria Jean to retire from Hollywood, she gladly accepted the position as receptionist for our guests, vendors, international and domestic distributors. She was the best as being the "director of first impressions."

I took a seat in the lobby as I waited for Gloria Jean to direct me to Paula's office.

Walking into Paula's office I was immediately struck with how feminine and colorful the décor. As she was a redhead, muted peach colored the walls, floor, chair coverings as well as the lighting. It was most flattering to her and to anyone who walked into the room.

Her desk was an ornate French provincial table with two wingback chairs facing her. An extraordinarily large painting of an ethereal woman hung on the wall behind her. Just below it, a table with just a few photos, key among them her husband, John Meehan, the president of REDKEN.

John had previously represented <u>Modern Beauty Shop Magazine</u> (now <u>Modern Salon</u>, the preeminent trade magazine in the salon industry). He was the West Coast Sales Director and called on Paula personally to convince her to buy advertising space in the magazine.

His visits to her office produced a relationship that not only put the growing REDKEN Laboratories in the hands of hairdressers, but placed John central in her heart. She was Yin he was Yang. She was creative he was pragmatic. She dreamed big picture he planned details. A great team. A good match. A vital couple for our industry at the time.

One defining day was when John walked into her office and opened <u>Modern Beauty Shop</u> to the centerfold and a two-page Clairol ad. "If you want to be as big as Clairol, you've got to look as big as Clairol in the magazine." At the time Clairol was top of their game, number one in the industry in this country and buying major ad space.

Paula's REDKEN was still up-and-coming lacking the funds to finance such a major business decision. Ultimately John's persuasion and her sixth sense to take his advice to publish "informational advertorials," she mortgaged a property and bought the ad space.

Rather than simply publishing new product introductions, she would publish the science behind the product and why it would improve the health of the hair and scalp.

Hairdressers flocked to this new way of meaning, new ways to grow.

I took my seat across from Paula with trepidation still questioning why she would want to single out a rookie field rep for a meeting.

Besides carrying in my Day-Timer in the event she wanted to see my day to day schedule, and my purse, I also carried a Gideon Bible borrowed from my Sheraton Universal Hotel room.

At one point in the meeting, I felt directed to ask her permission to read the passage from the gospel of Luke and explain how I believed my being employed with REDKEN Laboratories was a Divine appointment.

She sat riveted.

I began my story. It was in the previous October in Portland, Oregon in the latter part of my formal REDKEN training, I was attending my first seminar as a new field representative. It was Saturday night as I was preparing for bed that I began to question, "Is this new career what God really wants for my life?

I was ready for God's perfect will for purpose and fulfillment. If this job was simply feeding my ego and keeping me on the road in strange hotel rooms, driving across the country in the dark of night, and meeting strangers every day of my life, I wasn't so sure I was interested.

I snuggled into the warmth of the blankets feeling my body giving way to the pull of gravity as I released the cares and concerns of the day. There came the familiar sense of falling into that 'twilight zone' - that space between being awake and asleep. I 'heard' the Holy Spirit's still small voice in the recesses of my mind, "Look," it said.

"Look?" I thought. "Where do you want me to look?" I lay there silently anticipating the next nudge.

"Maybe 'look' means Luke. Maybe there's someplace in Luke I'm supposed to look."

Then in the silence, as if written on a white board just inches from my closed eyes, the numbers came 4 - 1 - 7. By not dismissing it as just a crazy thought, but following the guidance, I discovered the spiritual and scriptural foundation on which I would build my life's work.

Excitedly I turned the light back on, pushed back the covers and trotted over to the dresser drawer where I knew I would find a Bible placed by the Gideon Society. They are so faithful, the Gideon's. No matter where I've ever been in the world, on land, in the air, or on the sea, I've found solace knowing that I would have the companionship of the Bible by just opening a drawer.

I found my way through the New Testament, Matthew and Mark to Luke.

Then my heart started beating faster as I looked up the fourth chapter, seventeenth verse. I had no idea what I was about to read.

The scene finds Jesus in the Temple having just returned from the forty days and nights in the wilderness. He stood up to read scriptures from the Torah, Isaiah 61 recounted in Luke 4:17-22.

17) "The book of the prophet Isaiah was handed to him, and he turned to the page where it was written:

18) The Spirit of the Lord is upon me, for he has anointed me to preach good news to the poor; He has sent me to heal the brokenhearted; To uplift the downtrodden; To preach deliverance to the captives and recovering of sight to the blind;

19) To preach the acceptable year of the Lord.

20) And he closed the book and gave it to the minister. And the eyes of all of them that were in the synagogue were fastened on him.

21) He began by saying to them, "This prophecy has come true this day.

22) And they were amazed at the gracious words which proceeded out of his mouth.

Standing there, stunned, I closed the book and said out loud, "Oh no! I'm being called into the ministry and I don't want to do that!"

God knew I would be resistant, thinking that the only kind of ministry was to be a pastor in a small church somewhere and be the shepherd of a human flock.

Then again, His still small voice, "Ann, you are in the ministry. You'll be speaking to people who put all importance in the outer appearance. When they come to the seminars sponsored by REDKEN, they'll be expecting familiar presentations on hair and skin. You'll bring the perspective of inner beauty which is born of my love, joy, peace, patience, kindness, meekness, gentleness, self control."

The very attributes that serve as the source of a servant heart. The very kind of heart that the salon profession offers a hurting world. I accepted His calling through these scriptures as verification of my life's work. I had no idea at the time where the ministry would take me. I took to heart the message from Luke 4:17 and would become known as the spiritual advisor of my company and through opportunities to write and speak, ultimately throughout the salon industry as well.

Most importantly, in this moment with Paula, I was given the opportunity to share with her the depth of gratitude I had to her for this "mission field."

Paula totally understood.

That meeting marked the beginning of our 39-year relationship. It was a bond that went far beyond our business to a deep spiritual understanding right up to the final days of her life.

Paula modeled for me and other women how to not only be a "woman in business" but also to be a "lady in business." Paula's dynamic traits we emulated were her energy, enthusiasm and being the first to extend to others.

Although self-proclaimed a shy "lucky high school dropout." Paula would light up every room she entered with her bright blue eyes, brilliant smile and force of presence.

She was always asking questions, sincerely interested in what was happening in the field, what REDKEN was doing well, what we could do better.

She encouraged us, "If the decision you're about to make is in the best interest of the person standing behind the chair, JUST DO IT!" This was long before Nike took that phrase as its mantra.

Paula believed that every "knock" of the competition was a "boost," so we were reminded not to mention any of our competitors and to stay focused on what REDKEN had to offer; our science, our education, our inspiration. She was always encouraging us to never settle for anything lower than the highest; to be the best individually and as a company. As joyful, humorous and creative as she was, she could also stand firm especially as it related to defending our "salon only" commitment to retail. She was not afraid of litigation and prosecution of those who diverted our products to other retail outlets. Neither was she afraid to go 'dumpster diving' in the middle of the night to retrieve a distributor's discarded paperwork proving that diversion was taking place.

She had clarity and focus on producing products that would satisfy the needs of the salon and sell successfully through our distributor partners. To that end, she would pick up the phone and ask distributors for their opinion on a product or program and would listen intently and take notes. When the product or program was released the distributors would be her champions because they could see that their own ideas came to life. She asked, she listened, she delivered.

Paula held supreme respect for salon professionals. Her first and foremost dedication was to them. She recognized that everything she accomplished, all she accumulated and all the experiences of her life were due to the commitment of stylists standing behind the chair every single day using and recommending REDKEN products. She never took anything for granted and was beyond grateful.

Paula believed fully that the hairdresser was the single greatest resource for information on hair and skin. Salon professionals were elevated in the minds and hearts of their clients. She was dedicated to providing truthful products that would do exactly what they said they would do; to deliver a balance of protein and moisture at pH of 4.5 to 5.5. Exactly where nature intended them to be.

The "Scientific Approach to Hairdressing" and "Beauty through Science" gave stylists information, tools and techniques that increased their confidence in themselves, in their profession and in their ability to earn beyond their dreams.

As I discovered there's a big difference between having a job and having work. In my trainings across the globe I implore salon professionals to find their "work" while doing their job. Mine was defined by close encounters of a spiritual kind and by the guided words of REDKEN's Founder Paula Kent Meehan.

NUTRALON was a long shot. It didn't take us long to surmise that unlike our protein-based hair care products that were highly popular, nutritional supplements weren't going to be profitable for the salons nor for REDKEN. The minority of stylists who were enthusiastic about taking the supplements, weren't that confident nor interested in recommending ingestible products for their clients' nutritional needs.

Ultimately, the decision was made to discontinue the line, my line, and I would be out of a job. I was anxious about everything - which is contrary to the promise written in the verse printed at the beginning of this chapter. What was I going to do?

I went to Paula.

In her visionary way she spoke to me the words that would change my life forever, *"Change your message from 'you are what you eat' to 'you are what you think' and present motivational and inspirational messages to hairdressers."*

In those days there were few women on the manufacturers' education stages - with the rare exception of hair colorists, permanent wave specialists or the occasional haircutter. The main presenters were charismatic men who were smart and funny and appealed to the predominantly female - oriented audiences. They were very successful in selling our concept of "Beauty Through Science" and the products that solved clients' problems.

Then I appeared on the scene creating and presenting programs for stylists to focus them on their personal and professional goals. I recall the first presentation in this new arena, scheduled to appear with our business seminar team, "The Challenge of Success." We were in Cambridge, Massachusetts.

I created an acrostic from the word BEAUTIFUL and attached an action step to each letter of the word.

11
BEAUTIFUL = BE YOU TO FULL
Be Yourself To The Fullest

B - Begin each day with time for you
E - Eat food that gives you energy

Y – Yes! to life
O – Open up
U – Unforgiving is aging

T – Touch in appropriate ways
O – Offer what you can give, and accept the offers of others

F – Face to face/eye to eye makes the connection
U – Utilize all your gifts and talents
L – Listen with all you've got
L – Love is all you need

I turned the focus from the stylist to the chair, always caring for the client, to the unexplored waters of caring for themselves first...then the client. It was new. And it met with welcomed reviews.

From that first presentation I began to find my "work" - to be an unconditional encourager to salon professionals.

Just a few months later I was in Washington D.C., invited by my friend Jane Caplan who was the education manager for Davidson Beauty Supply. At this program, Janie was giving me the opportunity to present a program solo.

Once again in my hotel room I asked for Divine direction for the program and for my life.

I pulled the drapes to make the room conducive to rest. I had no intention to sleep, but rather to focus on what the presentation I was giving the next day.

As before, the Holy Spirit's still small voice sounded clearly. I wouldn't say I could actually "hear" it, as if someone was actually talking to me. The voice was more a whispering hunch.

Opening the King James Version of the Gideon Bible tucked away in the desk drawer, turned to where He was directing, Old Testament, Jeremiah, Chapter 1 Verse 4.

4) Then the word of the Lord came unto me saying,

5) "Before I formed thee in the belly I knew thee; and before thou camest forth out of the womb I sanctified thee and ordained thee a prophet to the nations.

6) Then said I, 'Oh, Lord God, I cannot speak for I'm only a child.'

7) But the Lord said unto me, 'Say not I am a child. For thou shall go to all that I shall send thee, and whatsoever I command thee thou shalt speak.

8) Be not afraid of their faces, for I am with thee to deliver thee,' saith the Lord.

9) Then the Lord put forth his hand and touched my mouth, and the Lord said unto me, "Behold I have put my words in thy mouth.

10) See I have this day set thee over the nations and kingdoms to root out, and to throw down and destroy, to build and to plant."

There was no doubt after reading this scripture I was given confidence to perform my life's work by my saying "Yes." And I did. And I am. And will continue.

As my friend Chelle Watt has so beautifully expressed, "When I stand before God I want to say I used everything you gave me."

Or, as Bill Withers sings, "Keep on using me, until you use me up."

Whenever I have moments of anxiety that threaten to strip my confidence, I rely on the two powerful scriptures Luke 4:17 and Jeremiah 1:4.

The third affirming verse I received in 1986 further cemented the calling when I was led to read Philippians 1:6 written by the Apostle Paul.

"Being confident of this very thing, that He which hath begun a good work in you will perform it until the day of Jesus Christ."

Every presentation that I've made to groups on the planet, from Tokyo to Toronto; from Santiago to San Diego; from Atlanta to Anchorage; from Caracas to Cape town; from Sydney to Seoul have begun with quiet time where I read these scriptures, affirmed their truth, and surrendered that whatever needed to be said would be said.

There have been times when I was surprised at what I felt prompted to share. I believe I've been faithful to the promptings and opened up to share the good, the bad and the ugly.

If there's anything I've learned, it's that all of us have lived with feelings of insignificance, failure, and disappointment. When I've allowed these times of my life to bubble up in my presentations, a sweet acceptance of the group would wash across the room. As Zig Ziglar always admonished, 'everyone you meet is in some level of personal pain; physical, mental, emotional, financial, spiritual.' So when I let the groups know I experience what they do, we automatically bond.

There have also been instances when an audience member will thank me for something I've said, and I honestly don't remember it coming out of my mouth. I think many times the Holy Spirit prompts their own thoughts that seems like it's coming from me, and they'll give me the credit.

What I do know is that I now have the courage to speak my truth, what I've never allowed myself to say. And it's making a difference in the quality of my life and in others, proving what Tony Robbins says, "The quality of your life is in direct proportion to the quality of your communication."

Any time now, when I have trouble falling asleep, I take it as a nudge by the Spirit to read something specific from the scriptures.

Why am I sharing this with you?

I believe everyday conversation is a presentation. We can be in our "work" with each person that's brought to our path. The Holy Spirit prepares their hearts just as ours are prepared to receive them. And this is exciting.

Everything we have, and will have, comes through others. It's vital to remember to stay open, honest and inviting so that you can give them what they need in the moment, and you can receive what you need from them in the moment.

Our work is our spiritual practice.

I believe the time has come to move from the duality of "professional and personal life" to simply begin to live "life" and allow the Holy Spirit to live and breathe and move in each of us every moment of every day.

So you can see, from the early days of being anxious about everything, to a lifelong calling I have been led by powerful and truthful words of my friends Luke, Jeremiah and Paul and Paula Kent Meehan.

And so it was no surprise that my final conversation with Paula was of a spiritual nature, just as our first conversation was 39 years earlier.

It was just sixteen days before Paula passed that I was perched on her king-sized bed, within touching distance from the hospital bed where she spent most of her days. The beautiful peach-colored fabrications of her bedroom allowed for the reflection of the same color in her cheeks. Windows opened allowed for the California sunshine and breezes to seep in.

The previous February she had gotten a deep chest cold and her delicate lungs were doing their best to expel the carbon dioxide but her breathing was becoming more and more laborious.

It was now June 7th, I held her hand. In that quiet moment, while the nurses were checking her charts and home care givers were doing all they could to make her comfortable she spoke.

"Oh Ann, I've made so many mistakes in my life, so many mistakes."

Squeezing her hand I responded, "Paula, you don't have to live with the weight of those mistakes. God is here. He wants you to accept His peace. All you have to do is just say 'yes!'"

Turning her tiny face toward me she looked at me with those piercing blue eyes and blurted out, "Oh Yes! Yes! Yes! Yes! "

I asked her to say The Lord's Prayer with me, a prayer we had said together many times. She did word for word. "…..forgive us our debts as we forgive our debtors." At the conclusion of the prayer I knew that Paula was prepared for her next journey, what I didn't know is that her Heavenly flight would be just 16 days later.

While on vacation with my family in Washington DC, we had just emerged from the Spy Museum on Monday afternoon June 23rd. It was around 12:30 p.m. when my phone rang it was Reyna, Paula's personal care giver. Gently and sweetly she said, "Miss Paula has passed." As we continued to walk, Reyna shared with me some of the beautiful memories of the final sacred moments. Just then we were headed into the subway station and there on a wall, encased in glass were these words, "STAY FOREVER CONNECTED."

Of course, I immediately interpreted this as an assurance from Paula that she had heard those words we all long for God to speak to us, "Well done good and faithful servant."

Through these three words she was also asking me to make sure our REDKEN circle of friends would stay forever connected in her absence.

In a powerful dream I had following her passing she said to me, "Ann, I never, ever used to think about Heaven, and now it's all I think about!"

I know I will see her again.

12
RADIATE
You Are A Star Right Where You Are

"Do everything without complaining or arguing, so that you may become blameless and pure, children of God without fault in a crooked and depraved generation, in which <u>you shine like the stars</u> in the universe as you hold out the word of life." Philippians 2:14-16

In 1978, the first photos from the Pioneer 10 satellite were beamed back to earth, revealing for the first time images of the planet Jupiter.

Rich in design, color and formations, the photo was reproduced on the cover of a newsmagazine. I looked at it with one question, "where had I seen this before?"

I sifted through the hair research files at REDKEN laboratories then located in Van Nuys, California. I found my answer. It was a photomicrograph of a plug of skin taken from the hand of one of our research chemists. Under the powerful magnification of the scanning electron microscope, the image of the skin, to my eye, was identical to the image of Jupiter! I found science, in that moment, to be a part of the new home for my spiritual journey.

My heart raced as I quickly began reading about the atmosphere of Jupiter made of a blend of the same elements making the composition of skin and hair. Nitrogen, sulfur. I was discovering the personal truth in the quote from famed astronomer Dr. Carl Sagan, "We are made of star stuff."

I also discovered through the lens of the scope, we even look like star stuff.

Further, noted nutritionist Adele Davis admonished in her book, <u>Get Well Naturally</u>, "When you stand and extend your arms and legs, you form a five-pointed star." Think of it, all the atoms of the universe move out of the way so that you can live, thrive and shine in your unique space.

Jupiter in the interpretations of astronomers and astrologers pay homage to its influence of the higher mind, intuition, the highest version of ourselves.

I began to open my heart accepting Jesus' admonition in Matthew 5:14, ***"You are the light of the world."*** To have wholehearted, loving-kindness for myself! Just as I am. To stop the urge to get on with the next thing and to turn the addiction of 'becoming' to 'being.' And through the words, stories, practices of this book, I'm encouraging you to start where you are and claim your stardom.

No other person can be in your space as long as you are there. No other has the right to deliberately 'dim' the shine of your gifts, talents and personality by putting you down or making fun of you. No other gets to make you feel insignificant or unworthy. Because no other has that power.

In their book <u>Built to Last,</u> the authors Jim Collins and Jerry Porras emphatically state "that the power we give to others is our gift to them; and just as we give to them we can also withhold or retrieve that power whenever we choose."

It's no longer necessary or acceptable to live your life vicariously through the lives of others, whoever they may be. Celebrities in the world of movies, television, music, theater, sports or any other arenas are no more a star than you are.

When you say yes to your 'stardom' and the optimum place where your light can fully shine, you will then vicariously live through yourself. I love this thought.

You will contribute fully, feel fulfilled and earn the most that you can give generously. One of the lines from the song I wrote, ***"I Can Do Anything"*** says, "….if not to give, what good is wealth?"

From this place of truth and grace you have the privilege of encouraging others to shine as the star they are, too!

YOU ARE A STAR RIGHT WHERE YOU ARE

Learning is the discovery of the possible and I know it's possible to radiate at full wattage by giving attention to and balancing each of the five points of your star:

- ✓ Taking care of your body.
- ✓ Taking captive every thought that enters your mind.
- ✓ Caring for your relationships with divine kindness.
- ✓ Making the right decisions in how to earn, invest, give and spend your finances.
- ✓ Living in alignment with the Holy Spirit through forgiveness and gratitude for the unlimited Love energizing you to serve others.

Giving attention to and balancing these five points each day, with even the smallest intentions, allows us to be able to give our full, undivided attention to others. I want every person I'm connecting with to leave our interaction feeling loved and wiser. As the message board at Marble Church in NYC proclaimed, 'Love is Presence.'

Can we imagine actually allowing ourselves to radiate without feeling self conscious or self-centered? How would our thoughts, words and actions change if we genuinely allowed ourselves to accept the truth, "I am a star."

The day the possibility to <u>RADIATE</u> broke through my clouds of fear was in Kansas City, the Hyatt Hotel. It was the spring of the same year the hotel suffered a major structural collapse on prom night and many people were killed. In this same hotel my spirits collapsed by a rumor that was being spread around about me. One of my managers broke the news to me.

I stumbled in disbelief to my room, stretched out on the bed and began thinking of all the ways I could defend myself. I felt defeated. Then, just as the Fairy Godmother appeared to Cinderella in her disappointment of being rejected from those closest to her, a series of words began flooding my mind. I knew it wasn't the fairy godmother, it was my faithful God Father who spoke His words of comfort to my breaking heart.

I began to write what I was hearing and taking each word, each line separately, I saw the end to my despair and defeat. The decades of captivity in which I'd been held to the lie of comparisons and the ignorance of individual significance were now coming to a screeching halt.

As I completed the last word of the last line, I knew without a doubt that the rumor and my fear of it would pass. The truth was the promise held in the lines of the poem, Starshine.

> **LOOK ALL AROUND YOU AND SEE WHO YOU ARE**
> **LOOK ALL AROUND YOU YOU'RE A SHINING STAR**
> **WHERE DID IT COME FROM**
> **WHERE WILL IT GO**
> **NOBODY'S CARING LIKE YOU DO**
> **NOBODY KNOWS LIKE YOU KNOW**
>
> **LOOK ALL AROUND YOU YOU'RE WALKING ON AIR**
> **LOOK ALL AROUND YOU NOW'S THE TIME TO SHARE**
> **A NEW WAY OF MEANING**
> **A NEW WAY TO GROW**
> **NOBODY'S CARING LIKE YOU DO**
> **NOBODY KNOWS LIKE YOU KNOW**
>
> **ALL YOU CAN SEE YOU CAN CLAIM JUST BY SAYING**
> **"IT'S MINE"**
> **ALL YOU MUST DO IS BE WILLING EACH DAY JUST TO SHINE**
> **STARSHINE**
>
> **LOOK ALL AROUND YOU THE TIME IS AT HAND**
> **LOOK ALL AROUND YOU NOW'S THE TIME TO STAND FOR**
> **ALL YOU BELIEVE IN**
> **SOME SEEDS WILL GROW**
> **NOBODY'S CARING LIKE YOU DO**
> **NOBODY KNOWS LIKE YOU KNOW**

VOCAL - RHYTHM

ANN MINCEY

STARSHINE

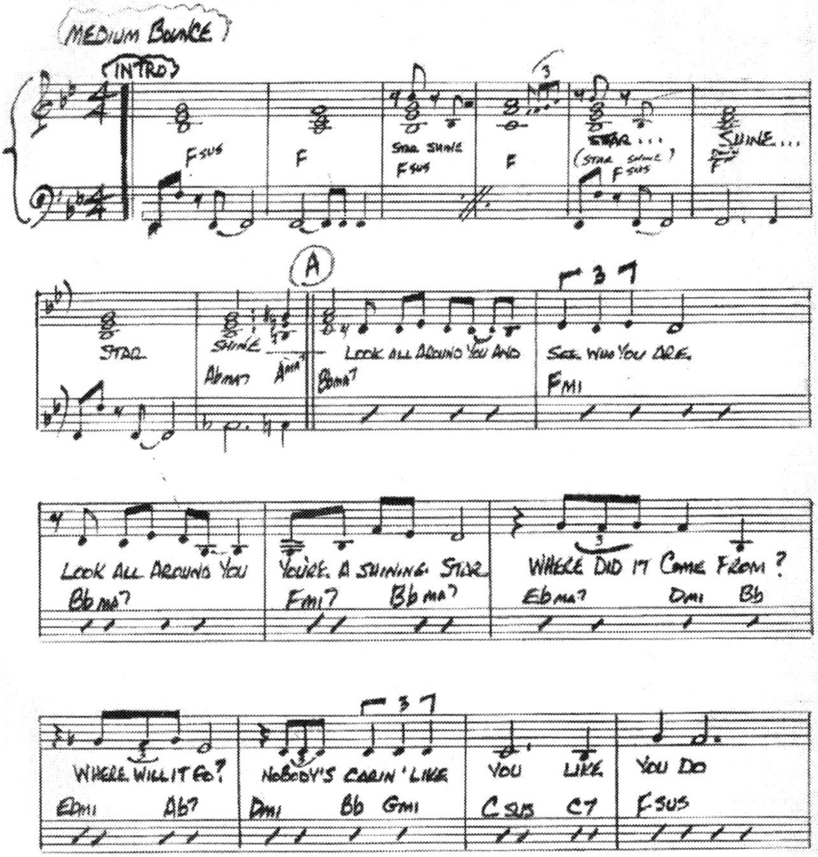

Piano-Vocal   STARSHINE   PAGE 2

NOBODY KNOWS LIKE	YOU			LOOK ALL AROUND YOU
Fsus	Fsus F/	Fsus	Abma7 A7	Bbma7

WALKIN' ON AIR	LOOK ALL A ROUND YOU	NOW'S THE TIME TO	SHARE
Fmi	Bb	Fmi7	Bb7

NEW WAY OF MEANING	NEW WAY TO GROW	NOBODY'S CARING LIKE	YOU... LIKE
Eb Bb	Emi Ab7	Dmi7 Gmi7	Csus C7

YOU DO...	NOBODY KNOWS	LIKE YOU			
Fsus	Fsus	Bbma7	Fsus	Bbma7	Absus/Bb7

ALL YOU CAN SEE YOU CAN	CLAIM JUST BY SAYING	IT'S MINE
Gma7	Emi7 G	Cma7

144

STARSHINE PAGE 3

All you must do is be willing each day just to shine

Star shine

Look all around you, the time is at hand, look all around you, now's the time to stand for what you believe in, what you can do, nobody's carin' like

VOCAL - RHYTHM
STARSHINE PAGE 4
YOU LIKE
YOU DO
NOBODY KNOWS
NOBODY KNOWS
NO ONE CARES LIKE
YOU
C SUS C7
FSUS
FSUS
FSUS
FSUS
LIKE YOU
KNOW
STARSHINE
FSUS
Bbma7
Db/Ab FSUS
Bbma7
Db/Ab FSUS
STARSHINE
STAR SHINE
Bbma7
Db/Ab FSUS
Bbma7
Db/Ab FSUS
REPEAT TILL FADE OUT

It is not my purpose to suggest that we declare and live our 'stardom' for its own sake.

Shining as the star that you are is the first step in serving. To serve is to be number one. The last is first. To accept that you're worthy to serve, and willing to serve without reserve, begins by accepting your significance and that begins with radiating the truth that You Are A Star Right Where You Are.

If you've had difficulty making yourself a priority please stop here and repeat silently, being aware how you feel when you say to yourself...

"I AM A STAR"

Now repeat this truth out loud inserting your name

I _____ AM A STAR."

13
BODY RADIATES
You Are a Star Right Where You are

"Are you tired? Worn out? Burned out on religion? Come to me. Get away with me and you'll recover your life. I'll show you how to take a real rest. Walk with me and work with me - watch how I do it. Learn the unforced rhythms of grace. I won't lay anything heavy or ill-fitting on you. Keep company with me and you'll learn to live freely and lightly. Matthew 1: 28-30

I must take care of my body. It is the reflection of what Christ is doing in my being to make me 100% like Himself.

INSPIRATION RIDES ON THE BREATH

When it comes to the issues of the body, so often we receive messages imploring us to take some kind of action; aerobicizing, stretching, weight training. While all activity leads to strength and balance and is beneficial, emphasis needs also to be put on resting, restoring and renewing.

Simply breathing is a great place to start.

In Genesis, chapter 2 and verse 7 it reads, "Then the Lord God formed a man from the dust of the ground and breathed into his nostrils the *breath of life*, and the man became a *living soul."*

Breath is Life.

On a flight across country, the gentleman sitting next to me stayed to himself, thankfully, until we were about to land in Los Angeles.

He finally broke his silence by saying to me, "I know what you love to do more than anything else."

I was a bit startled, thinking that he was coming on to me and not wanting any part of it. However, I responded by simply asking, "And what would that be?"

"Breathe."

I had to laugh and agree. The one thing that all of us ultimately love to do is breathe. So let's breathe.

- Just now, inhale a long, slow deep breath, if possible through your nose in to the count of 6. (1-2-3-4-5-6).
- Filling belly, lungs, chest.
- Pause to the count of three (1-2-3).
- Exhale through the mouth in a long, low warm sigh to the count of 6.
- Ahhhhhhh.
- Now again.
- In through the nose, filling entire torso with fresh, cool air to the count of 6.
- Pause to the count of 3.
- Exhale through the mouth in a warm sigh to the count of 6.
- Pause to the count of 3.

Now rest for a few moments in this pool of what Yogiraj Rod Stryker calls "unsurpassed calm."

The root word of inspiration is the word 'inspire' which means 'to breathe.' So when tired, creatively or emotionally blocked, my inspiration is as close as my next breath.

Long, slow deep inhalation, long, slow deep exhalation.

- "Breathe in Joy"
- "Breathe out Fear."

- ➤ "Breathe in Gratitude"
- ➤ "Breathe out Forgiveness"

- ➤ "Breathe in Abundance"
- ➤ "Breathe out Lack"

You will want to create your own list of positive feelings and/or emotions to contemplate as you inhale and exhale. Your choices could even include lines from a favorite song, a poem or quote.

One of my favorites is a great hymn that has perfect timing for inhale and exhale on each line. I repeat it three times.

> *"Breathe on me breath of God*
> *Fill me with life anew,*
> *That I may love what Thou does love*
> *And do what Thou will do"*

GUIDING BODY THROUGH A MOMENT OF RELAXATION

Read through the following relaxation technique. And then proceed. Even better, have a friend or loved one read through while you participate, and then switch to give them the same chance to relax. No solution eludes a quiet, expectant mind.

Close your eyes and tell your eyelids to relax. Did you feel your entire body going limp?

If not, tell your eyelids to relax again. Feel the release happening from your shoulders all the way down to the tips of your toes.

Ask your shoulders "where are you?" Drop them; allow gravity to release them. In stressful times, unconsciously shoulders rise, carrying undue stress and tension.

Take a slow deep breath.

Now speak silently the words "unsurpassed contentment."

What does the word contentment mean to you? Can you define it without any notion of guilt or laziness?

The degree that you've allowed this relaxed feeling is the degree you allow yourself to feel contented. And to feel contented is to be in the present moment. A place where you can listen to your body, because your body knows what it needs.

- Begin a journey through your body being grateful to every part.
- Every cell, every tissue, every muscle.
- Be grateful for your hair, eyes, mouth, and teeth.
- Be grateful for your neck, shoulders, and chest/breasts.
- Your heart.
- Your lungs, stomach, intestines.
- Be grateful for your internal organs including your spleen, pancreas, adrenal glands and liver; your kidneys, bladder, spine, pelvis, reproductive organs.
- Be grateful for your hips, thighs, knees, calves, ankles, feet and toes.

Whatever state they're in, be grateful. Thank them for their faithful service to you. Speak kindly to your body. And speak kindly about your body. Breathe into that area that carries aches, pain, and tightness. Bring fresh breath, inspiration, to those places.

Now mentally retrace your body asking the question, "If God's highest version of my body is that of a temple, what does my body need to keep it maintained as the Temple that it is?"

Stay quiet. Listen as you receive the answer. Acknowledge the urging and devote yourself to take care of it more, better, or differently.

You may be prompted to select different kinds of foods. It may begin to give you an appetite for those foods that will serve you better.

You may be prompted to drink more water, take a compliment of nutritional supplements or simply get outside and get a breath of fresh air.

You may be prompted to get more sleep. Or take rest breaks, what I call 'joy breaks' during the day.

You may be prompted to invest time and money on your eyes to improve your sight; your teeth to improve your smile and your digestion; your spine to improve your posture and circulation; your feet to improve your stability and agility.

You may be prompted to play!

The body is coagulated thought. To change your body is to change the thoughts you have about it, and the ways you habitually speak about it. "My big thighs, flabby arms, wrinkled face." Changing the thoughts and speech will give your body a greater chance of changing.

Before coming out of your relaxed state, have your friend read the following lyrics to a beautiful song, **"A Quiet Place"**, written by Ralph Carmichael.

> *There is a quiet place far from the rapid pace*
> *Where God can soothe my troubled mind*
> *Sheltered by tree and flow'r*
> *There in my quiet hour*
> *With Him my cares are left behind*
> *Whether a garden small*
> *Or a mountain tall*
> *New strength and courage there I find*
> *Then from this quiet place*
> *I go prepared to face*
> *A new day with love for all mankind*

Can you picture still water? Can you picture flowing water? Can you picture still, flowing water?

I never knew this could be possible. Only until I visited the unfathomable Isamu Noguchi "Water Stone" at New York City's Metropolitan Museum of Art. I could never have comprehended that water could flow over the stone fountain almost invisibly. It does.

This image is what I can **be** as I come from this 'quiet place.' While life's dramas happen my attention often gets caught in the flow. So I don't notice the stillness. With God's peace my heart can rest in the quiet place, to know that "everything is perfect and I'm grateful" remembering "no matter what's going on, God is in charge." I may not be able to see how He's in charge of the flow, of what's happening *around* me, but I can allow Him to be in charge of what's going on *inside* me to find the stillness.

Finding time to enter your own personal quiet place creates 'resting awareness.' It is here that God heals, inspires, guides and enlightens.

To change my body, I take a few moments to get quiet, relax and ask questions like "How can I take care of my body better than I have been?" I speak to my body kindly and I speak about it differently. If for instance I feel Divinely directed to get to the gym, such as lifting weights to increase muscle mass and improve strength, I use positive words rather than numbers to count.

Instead of silently counting 1-2-3-4-5-6-7-8-9-10-11-12 in my quest for toning and defining, I choose 12 positive words that will strengthen my resolve such as the beautiful nine Fruit of the Spirit ~ Love, Joy, Peace, Patience, Goodness, Kindness, Meekness, Self control. I find myself silently repeating these words as I climb and descend stairs, or any other time I have a need to count.

14
THOUGHTS RADIATE
You are a Star Right Where You Are

"Do not be anxious about anything...finally, whatever is true, whatever is noble, whatever is right, whatever is pure, whatever is lovely, whatever is admirable - if anything is excellent or praiseworthy, think about such things. Philippians 4:6-9

I AM WHAT I INTEND

Inspired Intention - Talking to the person inside of me that's scared - Giving her confidence for interaction

Have you ever had thoughts of inadequacy? I have. Sometimes I still do. What I know for sure is the attitude I choose effects my effectiveness.

I will never possess what I'm unwilling to pursue.

There's one time in particular that I learned a way to separate my SELF from my fearful thoughts and surrender to the truth.

It happened while visiting New York City. A traditionally intimidating environment in and of itself. This was more than 20-years ago, before Joan Lunden was named the new co-host of Good Morning America on ABC Television Network.

I mustered up the confidence to call the producer of the show to inquire about auditioning for the co-anchor position.

I believe, when we have an idea, we are also given the power to take action on the idea and make it come true. I believe this because the

Divine urge is God nudging me to admit "I'm ready for the highest and greatest experience of God through me."

I dialed 411 for directory assistance proceeded to dial the number I was given. The ringing began on the other end of the line. Suddenly, I was attacked with a severe case of "What Ifs."

- ❖ "What if…. they think I'm stupid."
- ❖ "What if…. they want me to leave my job at REDKEN and move to New York."
- ❖ "What if…. they ask what broadcast experience I've had."

With every ring of their phone the anxieties mounted.

I quickly hung up before anyone could answer.

Stepping away from the phone I began to rebuild my confidence saying "What's wrong with me? I speak to people all the time. They can't even SEE me! What am I so afraid to make this call?"

Have you ever lived this same drama? Do you know what I was feeling with my heart pattering and my hands clammy? When was it? What issue were you dealing with and how did you resolve it?

A book that I'd recently finished, prior to this trip, was entitled <u>Big You Little You</u>, by Grace Kristen and Richard Robertiello. It was a guide to finding and befriending the five-year-old child who lives inside. That child influences us more than we can imagine when it comes to asserting ourselves in unfamiliar experiences.

I pictured my five-year-old Annie.

The image was comical. Her mommy would cut her hair over the kitchen sink using sewing scissors.

The easiest style was a Dutch-boy, straight banged-bob that was shampooed with Prell on Saturday nights and neatly bobby-pinned on each side so there would be a bit of curl for Sunday morning.

At two years old, she tripped on sister's plastic dishes on the basement steps and tumbled down escaping injury except for the missing tooth that took forever to be replaced by her big girl tooth in front.

In addition, Annie spoke and sang with a lateral lisp. This meant that when she would say the "S" sounds it would slip from the sides of her mouth and often spray spit over anyone near her. Her lisp was the source of embarrassment. It gave her friends a great reason to make fun of her.

Poor little Annie. A Dutch-cut hairstyle with the side curls sticking out, a missing tooth in front and a juicy lateral lisp.... this was the child calling <u>Good Morning America</u>.

That day in that hotel room I was determined to work through the anxious thoughts of Annie, and I acted on the advice of <u>Big You Little You</u>.

Slowly, gently I began at my feet and visualized lifting Annie out of my body and setting her on the chair in front me. I stepped around in front of her and knelt down. Looking at her softly in her big eyes, I began speaking to her.

> "Annie,
> Honey I love you very much and I know you're afraid
> to call Good Morning America. It's ok for you to be afraid
> because you're little and you don't know how to talk to big
> people. But I do. So I want you to stay here while I go to the
> phone and make the call. When I'm finished I'll come back
> and get you, okay?"

I visualized Annie sitting there rubbing her teary eyes and swinging her little chubby legs. "OK," I imagined her to whimper. I went to the phone; the adult Ann picked it up and dialed the number.

This time I let it ring. This time I let them answer. This time none of the "What ifs" distracted me. This time I simply followed the Divine urge.

I didn't get the job. Obviously.
I know that really wasn't the point.

I believe God simply wanted me to know that I could separate Annie's childlike anxieties from taking action on the ideas He plants in my heart. Do you remember what you looked like in Kindergarten? Picture that little five-year-old and know that he/she lives within you still.

Where have you been procrastinating because of possible childlike fear? Can you picture your child sitting in front of you? Can you imagine speaking words of love and comfort to him/her? Can you see yourself proceeding to do what the adult in you longs to do?

I remember Wayne. He was fired from his job and spent the next three weeks wallowing in self-pity. He didn't get out of bed. He thought he couldn't face the day.

One morning the story of Annie - which he had heard me tell years before - popped into his mind. He called to tell me his story.

"I remember getting out of bed and walking to our living room where we had these great, overstuffed chairs. I lifted little Wayne out of my body and sat him in front of me, just as you had told us to do.

I told him I was going up to my office to make some phone calls and would be there until I scheduled three appointments for job interviews. I told him to sit there until I came back successfully completing the task that I had been fearful of doing before. And then Ann," Wayne continued, "I turned the television on for him to watch while I was gone! It didn't take long. I was soon back downstairs, rejoined my adult SELF with little Wayne. In a short time I was working again. Happy and productive."

"Whenever I feel afraid I hold myself erect and whistle a happy tune and no one will suspect I'm afraid...." So go the lyrics from the "Whistle a Happy Tune", a great song from <u>THE KING AND I</u>. The happy tune I 'whistle' is the sound of myself speaking to my inner child. When I feel afraid to take action, I'm reminded that those thoughts come from my child within.

The child within will always be with me. Now I have a method so I can see and talk to him/her, calm their fears. I have the choice to either allow them to paralyze me with their thoughts generating from fear.

Thoughts of impatience, nagging worry, doubt, tension, guilt, lack, judgments, criticism, cynicism, jealousy, envy, inadequacy OR it could be my adult taking action from a place of love which generates life, beauty, order, generosity, abundance, service, grace, humor, dignity, forgiveness, honesty and gratitude.

There are only these two - Love and Fear. The most important thought I'll ever have is the one I'm having right now. Is it coming from Love or Fear? I remember **Love eliminates Fear.**

The present moment is the only moment when Love is fully engaged. Fear dwells from the remembrance of past: Doubt dwells from the shadowed expectation of the future...the what ifs.

However, if I'm afraid of tomorrow I may not realize the past is just as dangerous.

Right now I ask myself this question: "How fully can I be in the present?"

The more fully present the more fully loving. The more fully loving the more fully serving. The more fully serving the more abundantly gifted with confidence to act.

It's MY choice. Love or Fear.
I choose Love.

Where I am on my journey has been flavored by the dominance of one of these two choices. That is all.

The conditioning with which I was raised caused impressions on my young mind. The impressions have created a lifetime of desires - every thought is a desire. So whatever dominates my thinking dominates my desires.

My desires move me into action. And my actions cause the continuation of my impressions and reconfirming my conditioning.

It's a cycle. And if it's working for me and the "mirror" of my life is showing me what I really, really, really want to see, bravo! If it isn't, then the cycle needs to be interrupted permanently, somehow, someway.

In the high performance team training offered to the senior management team on which I sat, the trainers from Guttman Development Strategies have used the following description to make this same point. "A core limiting belief is a STORY I tell myself that sabotages my ability to get what I want."

I'm beginning to be more and more aware when I repeat a story that's keeping me stuck in a particular life stage or lifestyle.

I'm also aware when I hear anyone around me telling their stories and I can quickly see how they're stuck in their own level of pain.

A story very often will begin with, "I can't…." "It's just my luck…." "What works for me is…" or any "I am…." statement.

I believe in asking the Holy Spirit to make me aware in the moment, of the old, worn out impressions and conditioning; to hit the delete button on my thought computer.

I want Him to replace them with the highest version He has in mind for me. It is then my responsibility to be circumstantially aware of His guidance in everything relating to this new version.

This way is the only lasting way to break the cycle and guarantee that I'll come from love for others and myself in all my desires and thoughts.

TODAY MY WORLD IS STRONGER
TODAY I CAN NO LONGER
BE SILENT ABOUT THAT
INSIDE THERE'S NO DOUBT
TODAY
I CAN DO MORE FOR YOU TODAY.

TODAY MY FUTURE'S BRIGHTER
TODAY THE LOAD SEEMS LIGHTER
FOR ALL THAT I KNOW MAKES ME
KNOW THAT I KNOW
TODAY
I CAN DO MORE FOR YOU TODAY

I AM UNCOVERING THINGS THAT ARE HIDDEN IN ME

I AM DISCOVERING EVERYTHING THAT I CAN BE
AND WANT TO BE
I FEEL SO FREE

TODAY MY WORLD IS CARING
TODAY MY WORLD IS SHARING
IT'S GREAT BEING ME
ALIVE
RICH
AND HEALTHY
TODAY
I CAN DO MORE FOR YOU TODAY

Vocal - Rhythm   Ann Mincey

TODAY

Slow Latin Feel

Gourd solo / Add Castinets / Cowbell, Bass Tom, Timbales etc.

Add Bass

To-day my world is stronger, to-day I can no longer be silent about inside there's no doubt to-day... I can do more for you to-day my future's brighter, to-day the load seems lighter all that I know lets me know that I know to-day I am un-covering things that are hidden in me...... I am dis-covering every thing that I can be and want to

VOCAL - RHYTHM
TODAY PAGE 2
G7
Db
BE I FEEL SO FREE TO DAY MY WORLD IS
Db C Bbmi
Gb
CARING TO DAY MY WORLD IS SHARING IT'S GREAT BEING ME A-
B7
Db
LIVE RICH AND HEALTHY TO DAY I CAN DO MORE FOR YOU TO- DAY
(INSTRUMENTAL)
Db
Bbmi
Gb
Ab7
Db
DR. FILL
Db
Bbmi
TO- DAY TO DAY TO-
Gb
(TACIT)
(VOCE SOLO)
F
BAND IN LAST CHORD
DAY I CAN DO MORE FOR YOU TO DAY...
fine

15
RELATIONSHIPS RADIATE
You Are A Star Right Where You Are

"Little children, let us stop saying we love people and let us really love them and show it by our actions." I John 3:15

Where do my deep gladness and the world's great hunger meet? The surrendered Self is the secret to life. Listen attentively, care deeply, love profoundly.

The first love affair is the one where I fall in love with mySELF. I look and find what's right and I grow in awe of the experience of life as the unique expression of God as me.

The greatest expression of this Self-love is to find the right fulfillment of time for myself and those closest to me...letting the rest of the world fill in the blanks after that.

My friend and colleague Peter Mahoney of Halifax, Nova Scotia has taught me much about this by telling his own story.

He was type-A all the way, working 16-hour days, smoking all day long and 30 pounds overweight. His marriage was in jeopardy, his children living day after day without meaningful connection with their dad.

Through a series of events Peter made a conscious choice to truly love and respect himself. He found himself staring at the calendar of the New Year that was just about to begin. He thought, "What are the things in life that would bring me happiness?" And he began to list them.

- ✓ Spending time with my kids.
- ✓ Running.
- ✓ Having time with friends, laughing, and enjoying each other.
- ✓ Taking 10 weeks' vacation with my family.
- ✓ Getting healthy.

Peter found himself plotting those activities into the calendar and making a commitment to stick to the plan as best he could without distractions. After he was finished he then said, "OK world, now you can have the rest of me."

He stopped smoking. Lost weight. Although his marriage ended in divorce, his time with his children increased. He began running and has successfully completed more than one marathon.

His running partner became his life's partner. And his businesses exceeded the annual projections.

Peter taught me to do this, too. First determining my values and visions for my life and then making the 'appointments' with myself to satisfy them and see them accomplished.

The second love affair is the one where I fall in love with others. Mother Teresa said it best, "If I spend time judging others, I have no time to love them."

LOVING OTHERS AS MYSELF

Ever since I was little, I remember a Bible verse that read, "Love your neighbor as yourself."

I thought it meant that my capacity to love you is equal in proportion to the love I have for myself. And that may be the way to translate the Master's words.

A greater reality came to me one day when I discovered a new way of interpreting this same command --"Love your neighbor as your SELF."

Actually when I look closely into the eyes of another person I can see my SELF in the dark center, the pupil, of their eyes. I may be looking at them, but I'm seeing myself.

I remember I'm not there to change who they are. I'm only here to give them what they want. What they want is to be loved, recognized and remembered. They want to be affirmed they are exceptional, essential, and equal. They want to belong. The very same as my SELF.

When sharing a moment with someone I often silently say to myself, "This person matters. What they're saying matters. How they're feeling matters. There's something important at stake here." I intend to develop the conversation in the way they can't say "no" to my relationship to them, because I'm giving them exactly what they want. Love, recognition, remembrance and belonging. With these, I bring them into a place of peace.

This kind of undivided, individual attention creates an interaction that can change a course of action. It's rare to have someone's complete focus in a day when it's easy to become distracted. When someone recognizes and remembers me, new life is breathed into me. I feel for those moments that I truly am alive!

To give that kind of attention is the result of my physical, mental and emotional freedom points aligning. To give this kind of attention comes naturally when I've accepted that I am a star. There's no comparison with anyone, anymore. No more feeling inadequate. There's nothing to prove anymore, rather I spend my time improving these moments of life-giving attention.

One way I've experimented with improving my communication is in the area of eye contact. Although I find myself constantly wanting to make better eye contact when I'm talking, the more important contact is made while the other is talking. I developed the following theory after studying the principles of Neuro-Linguistic Programming.

We know the left-brain is dominant in thoughts of a linear nature, order, logic and verbal/numerical. The left-brain controls the right side of the body - the right eye.

The right side of the brain is dominant in emotional sensitivities, color, design, vision. The right side of the brain controls the left side of the body - the left eye.

Here's my self-proven theory. When someone is speaking to me of topics emotional in nature (family, feelings, spirit, and dreams) I concentrate on looking into their _____ eye. You're right.
Left eye since it is the path to the emotional side of the brain.

When someone is speaking to me of business, investments, or directions from point A to point B, I gaze into their _____ eye. You're right! Right eye since the center of logic lives there.

This makes so much sense to me. I've done it for years and have had people tell me when we're engaged in whatever topic that's important to them; they feel like I've crawled into their soul. Maybe I have. You can too.

The other piece of connecting that I've found helpful, is in shaking hands. Making sure I have a firm grip is one thing, but making sure the little webbed piece of flesh between the thumb and the forefinger is making contact with that part of their hand is important, too. Why? It's a pressure point to the heart. When I know my hand is touching this point, I'm touching their heart. They don't know why this handshake is different, but they sense it is.

There is only your relationship with your SELF that you see in the world around you. When you finally recognize that one magnificent truth, you recognize that relationship is everything.

A good question to ask yourself in the morning, "Who needs what I've got?" "Who's got what I need?" I then trust the Spirit to lead throughout the day. I'm aware of 'whisper signals' giving the answers.

Every conversation teaches me what I need to learn. Others accept me to the extent that I accept them. They open up to the degree that I open up to them. I look at that person as a mirror of my SELF. Instead focusing on my desire to dominate the conversation, I focus on their desires by asking questions and listening for my answers.

For example, instead of thinking "What is this discussion doing for me?" I focus on "What is this discussion doing for the other person?" "What is most important to me" becomes "What is most important to you?"

Instead of dominating and telling everything I know about a topic, I ask them what they know about it. There's something at stake here. These are effective ways to demonstrate that I am truly interested in developing the relationship.

GIVING THEM WHAT THEY WANT

We've heard at some point about the Golden Rule, 'do unto others as you would have others do unto you.' There've been those I've known whom, in my opinion, haven't fallen in love with them and see others as a mirror reflection. Therefore, what they think and feel about themselves produces a less than positive 'doing' to others.

I like adopting the Platinum Rule, which is simply, 'do unto others as they would have you do unto them.' How do I know what they would have me do unto them? I ask them! And then be willing to give it.

My dad always said, "There are five key words to success...give them what they want." My newest version of this is "Serve them what they want," going back to the earlier thought that they're looking at me with "serve us" in their eyes.

Keep in mind everyone is interested in talking about what he or she does, who they know and where they've been. You can tell what thrills someone most; it's the first thing out of their mouths the first minute you're together. Anything they bring up can open a conversation because they never tire of talking about themselves.

Tell me what you long for and I'll tell you who you are. In <u>Love Languages</u>, Gary Chapman has identified the best ways to connect with how someone 'feels' loved. The five choices are (1) Quality Time (2) Gifts (3) Touch (4) Words of Encouragement (5) Acts of Service.

Breathe each of these expressions of love into yourself. Which one comes up as your priority? Express that to those closest to you. Let them know. Ask them the same question. When we know what it takes for those in our circle of concern to feel loved, and when we're willing to give that to them consistently, our bond with them grows richer, fuller, and deeper.

LISTEN! Your quality of life depends has much to do with how well you listen and how curious you are about others. Tony Robbins, famed change-agent says, "The quality of my life is in direct proportion to the quality of my communication."

We commonly assume that communication means talking. The best communication is when we're listening.

My friend Steve Shapiro made a lifetime study of what he called <u>The Miracle of Listening</u>. What I've learned from him is contained in his book and is a simple, two-part secret to great conversation: ASK! LISTEN!

Steve also reconfigured the word LISTEN to form two other practices that will engage another person fully.

LISTEN – SILENT– ENLIST

These three words speak volumes. First he compelled us to have the intention to Listen; then be silent as you listen; and finally enlist the other with your attention.

Listen specifically for personal information that sneaks into the conversation. For instance, when my friend Flora told me she and Joe, her husband, would be celebrating their 35th wedding anniversary on November 30th, I made a mental note. Later, I wrote the date in my book so I can follow up when the time comes and send a card or flowers. Catching those bits of information in your 'heartnet' as they're casually mentioned in conversation then following through does wonders for relationship.

Be curious by probing into the comments they say you can help them uncover more about why they feel the way they do, or what they truly crave. As you make a point to be curious, the conversation will lead to other topics of interest. This gives the cue to others you are involved in and actively listening to what they're saying. This, too, will bind your relationship richer, fuller, and deeper.

> **RETURNING CALLS PROMPTLY**
> **TAKING TIME FOR YOUR FRIENDS**

I love the phrase, "people are more important than projects."

When someone comes into my office and I'm busy at work, I stop. Most times they'll say, "I'm sorry to interrupt you…but…." Or they may ask if they're interrupting me. My answer is always "no." I won't let them feel rushed. I avoid whenever possible any distractions or interruptions while we're together, such as phones ringing or e-mails waiting to be answered.

My undivided attention gives them the feeling they are my priority. People aren't an interruption to my business people are my business.

A good story to illustrate this happened not long after I moved to New York. I found my place of worship at Fifth Avenue Presbyterian Church, located at 55th Street and Fifth Avenue. One beautiful summer Sunday morning, sleeping longer than I should have, I rushed to get ready for church. I threw on a little hat instead of doing my hair and took off. I rushed as fast as my legs would carry me up Lexington Avenue. I passed an obvious homeless person leaning against the outside wall of a local deli. When he saw me he said "Nice hat lady." Thrusting a dirty paper cup he was holding toward me, he continued, "cup of coffee, ma'am?"

Not wanting to be bothered or to break my stride, I casually said over my shoulder as I passed him, "Not today, I'm late for church."

The traffic light changed and as I was walking cross Lexington Avenue the Spirit began speaking to me in near audible tones, "What are you doing?"

The light changed again and I found the voice continuing as I stepped off the curb and continued to cross the street, "You're rushing to church to hear one more sermon on …. if you've done it unto the least of these my brethren, (the light changed and I crossed the street) you've done it unto me." When the voice stopped, I found myself standing in front of the man again. I had completed a square - across Lexington, across 55th, again crossing Lexington and again 55th and back in front of the deli, the dirty cup, and the man.

I looked into his forlorn eyes and reached into my purse. I pulled out a couple of dollar bills and skimming his crusty hand, I gently placed them in his offering plate, the cup. "Have a cup of coffee, and a bagel, too!"

My mom calls these moments "Divine Interruptions." I definitely believe this one was. In responding to this Divine Interruption and following through with the action I knew I needed to take, I felt like I had been to church.

ALLOW GRIEF

I can easily be tempted to give advice, especially when it's not asked for. Making 'you should,' 'don't cry,' 'don't worry,' or 'don't be sad' statements help others suppress their true feelings. They forego the pain they feel and steer away from trying to solve their problems that are causing them grief. They begin to find their own answers and discover the first step they need to take. Most of the time all they want is to hear themselves talk about what is happening.

This behavior invites them to come to me with what they need because I help them discover the cause, the answer and ultimately what makes them happy.

Grief, resentment, suppressed feelings prematurely age us. Here's a great gift to give you, or recommend to someone who is stuck in grief. My counselor and friend Maggie Craddock, without whom I would've stayed stuck in my grief over a lost love, gave it to me.

Draw a hot bath, as hot as you can stand and pour into the water rock salt. Immerse yourself in the bath and stay there until the water begins to cool down. The salt draws out the impurities from your skin and somehow from your spirit. Dry off and wrap yourself in a warm, soft blanket. Now, crawl under your blanket or sheet on your bed, bury your face in your pillow and allow yourself to begin thinking of the problem that's causing your heart to grieve. Soon you'll begin to sob. The sounds that come from pure sobbing may startle you. Let yourself hear them. And sob until there are no sobs left.

In the morning you'll feel lighter. Cleansed. Fresh. Free.

Nothing happens until the tears.

FINDING SOMETHING TO COMPLIMENT

Sincerely complimenting something personal about someone - their eyes, skin, hands or clothing and how well they look in what they're wearing is a sure way to establish rapport, which can lead to a relationship. Rather than saying "That's a great dress." You now have a choice to say, "You look great in that dress." The truth is that each time you give a compliment to another person, you're also giving to yourself. Ralph Waldo Emerson wrote it best, "What we see is always ourselves." I would say on most occasions when I compliment someone, they'll blow off the compliment. When this happens, I literally make them pause a moment, I restate the compliment, and remind them to say a simple "thank you." In that instant their negative pattern of not allowing themselves to receive is broken.

Your relationships glowing are a new way to look at the Golden Rule. Pay attention to others as if you were others. In essence, you are others. In loving them, you love yourSELF.

APPRECIATING THEM AND TELLING THEM SO

When I appreciate my family, friends, colleagues I tell them so. Every time I see an opportunity to thank someone for something they've done, I do it. I stop, take a look at them eye to eye, touch them in some way and tell them how much I appreciate who they are and what they've done.

My friend Ron Mercer was a lifetime executive with Xerox. For part of his career he led the Canadian Xerox team. With only a few thousand employees, the Canadians were recognized with outstanding sales awards, out producing the major Xerox company in the UK.

I asked Ron how they accomplished this amazing feat. He replied, "We have a great team and they have excellent product knowledge. I guess if I were to boil it down to one thing, it would be that I appreciate my people and I tell them so. That includes the secretary, the maintenance crew that cleans the offices. Everybody. As they're leaving the office for the evening, I say, "Thanks for the day."

"I believe gratitude makes all the difference."

Appreciation takes what is great in others; makes it my own.

GIVE AND IT SHALL BE GIVEN

Another way to show appreciation is taking a small gift when visiting someone's home. I learned this from my friend Abraham Baghverdani, a college classmate who lives in Teheran, Iran. He would never think of entering a friend's home empty - handed.

Leaving something behind to remind them how grateful I am for our relationship extends our visit long after it's over and I've gone.

What I bring is not as important as bringing it. Fresh flowers or fruit, a greeting card with just the right message are lasting reminders. Showing appreciation and respect for others comes in ways that, over time, strengthen the trust and loyalty, the cornerstones of relationship.

FOLLOWING THROUGH ON COMMITMENTS

We've heard it and it's as true as ever. Under promise...over deliver.

One of my friends in the salon industry, Jon Prill, capitalized on opportunities and enjoyed great personal and professional success. I asked him what he considered the secret to his success. He thought for a moment and then replied, "I do what I tell them I'm going to do."

"That's it?" I questioned. He continued. "That's all they ask for. Most don't follow through with what they promise, so I've been ahead of the game and it's been profitable for me." So simple.

RETURNING CALLS PROMPTLY

Being prompt by returning messages whether on voice mail, e-mail or any other means, helps in developing relationships. In our lightning-speed world, where decisions and plans need to be made quickly, the 'urgent' return of a call just may be what they're waiting for to clinch an important deal or to simply progress with their plans. It may not seem that monumental to me. To them something very important could be at stake.

Sherry Lansing, former CEO of Paramount Pictures, stated on a Pacific Bell television commercial that she was committed to answering every day's phone calls by end of day. Those 30 seconds made such an impression on me as I thought "If Sherry Lansing can return daily calls with her busy schedule, there's no excuse for my not at least attempting to do the same."

Since then I've finished the day with most, if not all, phone messages - and now e-mails - returned. It feels good to know others aren't waiting for my input or response to proceed.

BEING FIRST

My most practical lesson from motivational speaker/author Zig Ziglar came in eight short words.

"If I'm not ten minutes early, I'm late."

It's a matter of respect. Showing up on time, being the first to arrive shows I have supreme respect for colleagues, family and friends.
I set my watch ten minutes fast and am the first to arrive to greet everyone. There's power there.

I'm first to express and extend my hand and a smile when entering a room, when meeting someone for the first time, or when there is a rift between me and someone else. It reminds me of what Blair Singer, one of the leading teachers and facilitators in the world taught me, "whenever greeting someone, the person with the most energy in the first two minutes wins!"

ENCOURAGING OTHERS

As I grow in the realization of my radiating Star, I'll soon begin to realize everyone has his or her special place to 'shine.' Their place, mission, talent has nothing to do with me. No one can keep my unique gift from me, nor could I or would I want to keep theirs from them.

With that in mind, it's easy and exciting to listen to others' triumphs and success stories to celebrate with them and encourage them on their way.

These actions take nothing away from my own star radiating. It bonds me to my relationships. It's so great to live free of the lie of comparisons. Because comparing is a lie.

The only comparison allowed now comes from Lloyd John Ogilvie when he implores us to 'stand at my full height and compare myself to God's greatness He intends for me to achieve'.

I'm reminded of a television commercial produced in the 1960's by Equitable Life Insurance Company:

> *"Is there anyone else in the whole human race*
> *With you kind of style and your kind of grace.*
> *There's nobody else exactly like you.*
> *There's nobody else like you."*

This truth becomes the core value of my life. It allows me to join in the encouragement and celebration of others. There will be times when I don't have any idea what a difference my encouragement makes. It could be a matter of life and death. As was the case of my two friends, David and Ron.

It was a sun-drenched day in California. The kind of day that Midwesterners decide to move from their bleak, blustery towns to feel the warmth of the sun almost 365 days a year.

I was returning from lunch and nearing the employee entrance to the building when I saw Ron. His carrot-red hair falling nearly halfway down his back. He worked on the sanitary production floor filling shampoos and other liquid products so most of the time it was worn back and up in a hairnet. However, it was lunchtime and he had taken it down allowing it to fly around in the warm breeze.

Passing him I simply said, "Hi Ron. Beautiful day!" He muttered something under his breath making his way to his car.

The following morning when I arrived at my desk, there was a cassette tape with a note scotch taped to it. I didn't recognize the handwriting. Opening the envelope and lifting the note out, I looked at the signature. It was signed 'Ron.'

Dear Ann,

Thank you for speaking to me yesterday as I was leaving the building for lunch. You'll never know what your kind smile and friendly words meant to me.

You see I was on my way back to my home to take my life. I didn't think there was anything to live for anymore and life was useless. Then I saw your face and heard your voice and I suddenly looked around. I realized "hey, you know what, it is a beautiful day." Rather than ending my life on that lunch hour, I began my life.

I've compiled a few of my favorite songs on this cassette tape that I hope you'll like. It's my way of saying thank you for your smile.
Sincerely,
Ron

Ron left his employment at REDKEN not long after that, finished his journeyman electrician training and became involved in the construction of some of the most beautiful skyscrapers in downtown Los Angeles.

How could I know that a smile and a positive word would have that effect on that day? I couldn't. That's why it's vital that we are balanced in our own glow so that we can be available to those who are brought in our path for encouragement.

David was another story of a man on the brink. I was in Canada teaching a class on personal grounding. David made his way into the classroom to simply find some peace and quiet. I'd chosen soothing music and dim lights to greet the learners and to put them into a receptive mood for the life-enhancing topic we were going to be talking about. He sat alone. Never spoke to another person. Shy I guess. What was going on inside him was the same unrest going on inside Ron.

Discouraged, disillusioned, dysfunctional. The class began with an exercise in relaxation. The group followed my instruction taking deep breaths "in with love, out with fear." Quietly I guided them through a relaxation technique with the objective of letting go of the stress that can so easily build up day after day in the salon.

Sometime in the course of the class, David heard me say the word "change." Just that. Change. Simple and direct. Like the flaming arrow that was lit and sent into the Olympic torch in Barcelona signaling the beginning of the Games, David heard the fiery word and it lit a torch within him.

The next day he sought me out to tell me what had happened. "Sitting there relaxed and quiet, I heard the word 'change.' I've heard that word thousands of times in the past, but today - the way you said it - I was struck that I must stop complaining and being disheartened by how I was living my life. I realized no one could do it for me. And in those brief moments, I made the decision to change. Forever change and never look back. You saved my life, Ann.

I was going to sit in your class and had already decided that when it adjourned I would go back to my hotel room and commit suicide. Instead, I met Holly."

That night in the Hospitality Suite this same shy David struck up a conversation with Holly. Her life was also in flux. A marriage that wasn't working, a salon struggling to be a real business. Together they talked about their current life status. And they talked. And talked. Into the wee hours of the morning they shared and laughed and cried. And they fell in love.

Within a few months they both had made the changes they needed to make in order to be together. They announced their engagement and had a beautiful wedding in the garden. Holly and David are like two giggly teenagers in love. They combined their lives, their families and their work. They know they were meant to meet each other at the REDKEN Convention. They also know they're meant to be together helping others find the courage and take action on the changes they so desperately need to make.

Recently I received a card David sent with a thank you note tucked inside from one of his clients. He had taken a few extra minutes during her salon service to give a soothing scalp, neck and shoulder massage. In her note the thank you was for more than just the tender touch. She said, "I've broken up with my boyfriend and haven't felt a kind touch since. Being in your chair made me feel like a woman again and I know I'm going to be all right."

David's gift to her was to let her be who she never thought she could be.

The stories are endless and the point is obvious. We are never aware of all the subtle gestures that we perform daily - without a thought - that are making an impact on those around us.

TOUCHING WITH YOUR HEART

Touching is helpful in developing a relationship. Periodically throughout the conversation, I reach out and touch. Even for those people who are shy about touching, a slight touch on a 'safe place' such as the upper arm between shoulder and elbow, is comfortable and comforting. They keep a physical connection between me and send a silent message to the other person, "I'm interested and I care about you."

In study of the energy meridians of the body, the heart energy makes its way through the shoulders, arms and hands. When I touch another I'm literally touching with my heart.

HUGGING

And for those we feel closest to and safest around...HUG! Hugs can be the refreshing break someone needs that can have lasting fond memories.

It's been noted that hugging can be a big help. Hugging is healthy because it improves blood circulation and relieves tension. Hugging combats depression and reduces stress. It's invigorating and rejuvenating. It elevates self-esteem, generates good will. Hugging has no unpleasant side effects. It's nothing less than a miracle drug!

I remember the first time I hugged my friend Chris. We were totally self-abandoned feeling the fullness of our bodies all the way from our shoulders to our toes.

When we released from the hug, I complimented him on his willingness to hug me so unselfishly. Chris' reply, "I have nothing to hide."

Maybe that the secret to giving and receiving not only hugs, but everything we desire. Nothing to hide!

Some may misinterpret the gesture of a hug. To avoid embarrassment in this regard, I've started asking; "May I give you a hug?" before I assume that it's all right with them. This is known as permission marketing and in today's business environment asking for a hug - or anything else you want - is a smart thing to remember.

Try this for a new sensation offered by my friend Chris. When you're hugging left shoulder to left shoulder, you're hugging heart to heart. Try it. It feels awkward at first. It puts a news spin on the sometimes-routine action of hugging right to right. What I call "self-abandoned" hugs being able to feel your body pressed fully against another's' shoulder to shoulder, chest to chest, stomach to stomach, pelvis to pelvis, thigh to thigh and toe to toe.

Wonderful!

With men, with women, few are willing to surrender and simply go for it. Those who do, know hugging is a great gift you give your SELF as well as someone else. And it makes you unforgettable.

LETTING GO

Knowing when to let go is one of the greatest lessons in relationships. Whether it's with a loved one, a child, a parent or partner, the code that you've made as the star that you are may sometimes require that you let go of someone who is no longer good for you or for your growth.

This point reminds me of a wrenching story of love and loss that offered the promise of the home I longed for.

As a twice-divorced woman in what is known as the prime of life at 50-plus, the idea of having a home had been on my mind. Not a drastic, obsessive thought. Just there.

When I received a call from a former college classmate I have to admit, I thought this could be a possibility.

For three and a half years, we conducted what would be considered a successful long-distance relationship in that it lasted well beyond the average lifespan of six months.

This man's lifestyle was filled to the brim with the activities of his beautiful ranch including the care of horses, cattle, and farm animals of all shapes and sizes. He owned property in Canada and Mexico, was in constant motion looking after the investments, as well as his family which consisted of his three growing children, his mom and sisters.

It was non-stop action with Robert and I did my best to keep up. Hunting trips to South Africa, calving in the middle of the night in sub-zero degree weather in Canada, hiking the rough terrain of the Rocky mountainsides. And much more.

From Fifth Avenue during the week to Dale Evans on the weekends, I did my best. And why? Because I thought this was the answered promise of home that I'd asked the Lord to provide.

Just prior to Christmas of 1999 and the highly celebrated Y2K New Years Eve taking us into the new millennium, I came to the startling realization that he was as committed to never remarrying as I was to marrying. So for me to continue with the fantasy was a violation of my value system.

"If you want a monogamous, committed relationship, I'm your guy," he told me as he sat in his overstuffed leather chair in the living room at the ranch house. I loved the privacy this place afforded. My kind of privacy away from the demands of my New York responsibilities and people, people, people. The house was nestled in the pines, the driveway 3 ½ miles long off the nearest paved road.

He continued, "But if you want to be married, I'm not your guy."

He had actually told me the first weekend I visited this glorious place, that he would never be married again, after two 'unfortunate marital experiences,' as he called them. But like most women, I thought he'd change his mind if I could just be enough.

He'd made his declaration early on. I just didn't hear it because I didn't want to hear it.

For the next three years I tried to be enough. It wasn't to be. And within a few days, I boarded a flight, said goodbye, and sang "Happy Trails to you." I cried all the way home.

I kept telling myself, "This is the BEST thing that could've ever happened." "This is the best thing that could've EVER happened." Did I believe it? Did I feel it? No, of course I didn't. I held the thought anyway. Day by day. Sometimes breath by breath. I was so sad. And yet in some strange way, I was relieved. I could breathe. And ultimately now, I can say, it was indeed the best thing that could've ever happened.

Why is letting go so difficult? It's a habit, a routine that has become part of the daily thought and action process. In order to change the familiar, new habits need to be formed. In our case, a hiatus of 90-days was declared with no communication at all.

I retreated to a solo vacation in the British Virgin Islands. Daily I'd take walks on the beach, write my cares and struggles in the sand and stand to watch the faithful tide take them away. It was my physical way of releasing everything to the Lord.

Reading Iylana Vinzant's book, In the Meantime, I adapted a practice that I found most helpful as I followed it to the letter.

I imagined inviting this man into my home. I was to ask him to sit down, and remain quiet. It was now my turn to say *everything* I was afraid to express because I didn't want to lose him. Since I had lost him, I now felt safe to express them. Off I went, out loud without hesitation, in my honesty and tears until every point was uncovered. When I finished I stood up, walked the imaginary 'him' to the door, and said a final "goodbye."

Of all the counseling, praying and journaling, this one practice cleansed this dear man of the powerful hold I had allowed him to have on me.

I left that vacation ready for a new life.

For seven months I felt the wrenching "pulling away" from the routine of daily phone calls, trips out west and the serenity of the ranch. I likened it to the same tug that happens when you pull the skin off the chicken breast before cooking it. Tearing away from someone you love is difficult. And possible.

We both know now it IS possible. I'm never settling for anything less, and I pray he hasn't either.

Again, I reached out to my saintly mother after the aftershock of this relationship ending subsided.

"Why is it that I'm the one to be the interim woman taking these wonderful guys who are in the throes of breakup, listen to them, love them unconditionally, and then when they're "rehabilitated" they find the "perfect puzzle pieces" in someone else and I'm alone, again.

She paused. And then quoted the words to the Heavenly chorus written by Hal David and Burt Bacharach, to put everything in perspective for me, once again.

In His time
In His time
He makes all things beautiful
In His time
Lord please show me everyday
As you're teaching me your way
That you do just what you say
In Your time
In Your time
In Your time
You make all things beautiful in Your time
Lord my life to you I bring
May each song I have to sing
Be to you a lovely thing
In Your time

ASK

There's one more point that I believe most women, and truly including myself, have a major hesitation and that's asking for help and then allowing ourselves to receive what others want to do for us.

Here's a great story that describes this beautifully.

We were preparing for the Marshall's Salon Services educational event in beautiful Lake Geneva.

The leaves on the trees outside the model room were already dressed in their fall colors, and inside the room, hair was being changed by design and color to demonstrate the new looks for the season.

For the third year in a row she arrived at model call, hoping that this time she'd be chosen for the makeover segment.

One by one, she saw the other women being interviewed, asked to wait for further instructions, or dismissed and thanked for coming. She knew that feeling and this year she didn't want to hear those familiar words, "Thank you for coming, but we're looking for a specific hair type in order to show the new looks."

"Please pick me, oh please pick me," she thought.

Finally the selection process was complete. Gary Harlan, the REDKEN National Performing Artist was leaving the room and he looked her way. Still planted in her chair, he asked her if he could help her with anything.

"I've come here for three years in a row and each time I've been sent away. I really want, I really *need*, a new look." Although quiet in her demeanor, she was bold in her request.

Gary took a look into her face. "Pretty," he thought. Although his initial impression of her hair was not one that he'd use for his presentation, he wanted so much just to do her hair and send her away.

"I'll just do it as a gift," was his thought. Little did he know that he was about to reorient the very core of her being. With this one opportunity he was going to make *the* difference in her life.

He had a Polaroid photo taken of her 'before' look and posted it on the signed model release form.

She was ushered into the model room where her hair was prepped for hair color. "Red," Gary thought, "she'd make a great redhead." He began to mix a formula that would bring out the best of her skin tone and eyes.

With hair still wet from the post-hair color shampoo and conditioning process, she was then led to Gary's partner, Flint Cross who began to cut and design her signature style. Letting go of length, the Indians believe with long hair comes old thought, with every close of Flint's shears she was cutting off old thoughts. Her hair began to respond to inspiration and she was thrilled.

The final stop after blow-drying and styling was the makeup chair and wardrobe. The look came together so beautifully that Gary and Flint decided to put her on stage with them as their finale model.

Presenting her to the audience was beyond a dream come true for her. On the large video screens at the front of the room was shown the 'before' Polaroid photo; a woman obviously downtrodden, oppressed.

A collective gasp and thunderous applause filled the room when she walked from behind stage down the runway. She stood and allowed herself to absorb the adulation. This was finally her moment. In the model room following the event, she thanked Gary and Flint with big hugs. Tears filled her eyes as she began to speak through the lump in her throat.

"I've never felt, nor have I ever been told that I was beautiful. Now I know that I am. I've been doing research in the last few months about women who are serving time in jail for killing their abusive husbands. I've been in an abusive situation for years and was seriously considering it. Now I realize I don't have to kill him, I just have to leave him. You've given me the courage to know that I can!"

Gary and Flint, just doing what they'd been doing weekend after weekend across the country - preparing for another educational event for salon professionals - took the time to care for a woman whose life would have taken a completely different course.

Except that she was determined to ask for their help, allowed herself to receive their gifts of making her look and feel beautiful, and ultimately, she was free to live in her new beauty.

For all of us, in the coming hours, let us be circumstantially aware of the opportunities we have to ask for someone's help. Breakthrough barriers of asking and open to others' privilege of asking me for my help.

"Do you know Oprah?" These were her first words Glendah spoke the minute she recognized my American accent and surmised that I was visiting Johannesburg on a business trip.

We were registered at Caesar's Hotel and Casino, the South African version of Caesar's Palace in Las Vegas. Our REDKEN team had invited leading salons from all over the country to join us for a two-day educational event and I was privileged to be one of the guest speakers.

Walking each day from the hotel to the convention area we'd pass through the array of shops and restaurants along the way. Glendah was the hostess at one of the more popular restaurants. My colleague

Debbie Miller and I stopped in for tea that first afternoon. It was then that she asked the question, "Do you know Oprah?"

Although I confessed I didn't know Oprah, I asked her what Oprah represented to her, a twenty-ish, bright, vivacious South African girl. "She's my idol," she said. "She's just so wonderful and one day I'll come to America so I can meet her."

Each day during our stay I visited with Glendah, as she would stand at the restaurant podium out in the openness of the passageway. We had our picture taken together and I handed my business card to her with these words, "If I can ever do anything for you to help your dream come true to meet Oprah, please let me know."

Upon my return to the States, I mailed her the photo with an encouraging word to follow her bliss. I asked her to stay in touch with me.

Within two weeks I received an e-mail message. Glendah wrote, "You told me to call you if you could help me in any way."

This was the truth. I recalled handing her my card with my contact information. "Yes," I said. "Did you think of something I could help you with?"

"Oh yes!" I could tell she was excited. "I want to go to college." "COLLEGE!" I thought, "Oh no! She wants to go to college and she's going to ask me to send her."

I probed. "Where do you want to go to college?"

"I want to be an airplane mechanic and I found a college here in Johannesburg, Kempton College, that has a two-year program and I wanted to ask you to help me go to college."

I drew a long, slow deep breath. "Glendah, you have a wonderful dream, and I'd love to help you become the best airplane mechanic. Tell me, do you know what the tuition is for such a school?"

"Yes, I already got all the information," she said in that beautiful South African accent reminding me of Meryl Streep in her role in <u>Out of Africa</u>, my favorite movie of all time. "It's very expensive," she continued.
I gulped and braced myself for the worst. "The tuition for the year is 3,600 Rand." I quickly calculated on the latest exchange rate at the time, nine rand to the dollar, this would be $400 US.

"Four hundred dollars," I repeated to myself. "This is such a small investment for such a great return." I quickly said, "Yes, I'll do it. I'll believe in you and your dream and I'll be happy to send you to Kempton College so you can become an airplane mechanic.

She organized her housing and enrolled in the college. I coordinated wiring the payment to her bank account, coordinated her registrations through e-mails, phone calls and faxes to the registrar. The total for her entire year's expenses was a rousing $1,000.

When I visited my bank to transfer the funds to the South African bank I was overjoyed to be able to help a young woman in another country realize her dream. All the paper work was complete. The funds were drawn from my account. I looked at the teller at my JP Morgan Chase Bank - where the right relationship is everything - and said, "Do you know what we just did?"

She looked at me puzzled still focused on stamping "paid" on the transfer paperwork. "What did we just do?"

"We just helped a girl in South Africa go to college!" I was thrilled. Tears filled my eyes.

"We did?" She asked with a satisfied smile glistening through her eyes.

Traveling back to Johannesburg one year later, I was determined to visit with Glendah and see the college she was now calling home. I phoned her cell and received her voice message, and when I told her where I was staying she knew it was within a few short miles. Hopefully we'd be able to make a plan to get together.

Two days passed. No word. I was getting anxious that something had happened to her. It wasn't like her not to call. I was finishing a morning of R&R in the hotel spa and as I was checking out, the reception phone rang and the receptionist handed the phone to me.

"This is strange," I thought. "Who knows I'm here?" On the other end of the line was one of my colleagues saying they'd been looking for me because my friend Glendah was at the hotel and had been wandering around for an hour or more looking for me. We finally connected.

We hugged and cried. She introduced me to her aunt and uncle who'd driven her to meet me. Then I invited her to lunch with me in the swank hotel restaurant. This is where the story got better for me.

We were seated at a table with a view of the verandah, a beautiful fountain, manicured lawn and swimming pool within our vision. We looked at the menu, ordered our lunch choices and the breadbasket arrived with a variety of sumptuous breads and rolls.

Soon enough, her spaghetti with meat sauce and my Caesar's salad with chicken arrived and we dove into the delicious conversation and the food.

She revealed that she came from a village in the Kruger National Park and was one of four children who graduated from high school. Her father was killed in an auto accident and mother was currently taking care of Glendah's three-year old daughter, Crystal, while she was in Johannesburg getting her education.

While she had been working at the restaurant where I had met her a year ago, she would send money back to her mother to help in supporting Crystal. However, since she was going to school full-time, the money was no longer available. I could hardly stand to think that these precious people were destitute.

"How do they live now?" I asked. She assured me about her mother raising vegetables, peanuts and maize and that's what they eat. Her determination to finish her schooling now was making more sense. She wanted to provide for her loved ones.

"Why airline mechanics' school?" I asked her. She could've chosen any field, including my own, cosmetology. She took a moment to answer.

"It's not so much that I want to work on airplanes. It's that I care so much for people and I want to make sure that when they fly on the airplanes that I work on, they will be completely safe." She continued, "There's a point at lift off and landing that is very, very dangerous. It's called the "angle of attack." This is the place where the aircraft is between making the commitment to the higher altitude and the earth's gravity. The hydraulics must work perfectly at the angle of attack. That's what I want to do, I want to be a hydraulic expert." Although I was trying to eat my lunch during this conversation, I found my mouth was open only to gasp at her compassion and wisdom.

We ordered dessert. She wanted the tri-color gelato and we both decided to go for it. More than once she commented that she couldn't believe she was eating in such a beautiful place.

The check arrived. As I was taking care of it, I saw her eyeing the breadbasket, still on the table, untouched. "Did you pay for that?" she asked.

"Yes, when you ordered your meal, the bread was included in the price. Do you want to take it with you."

"Oh. Could I? I would have one of those pieces of bread, or rolls, for breakfast each morning."

My heart sank. How many times have I dined in beautiful places and left the bread on the table. How often have I prayed the line in the Lord's Prayer, "give us this day our daily bread" and not given thanks for His provision every single day?

Here was a special girl who was teaching me so much about appreciation of what's in front of us, not taking it for granted and using what we've been given.

We took a car to the college campus and walked through the buildings, met the administrators, took pictures galore. She was proud to show it off, I was prouder to watch her in her element.

Glendah's story continued to inspire me. Her grades from the first year at Kempton College were more than acceptable. She passed with flying colors and was accepted to Denel Aviation Training Academy to continue her education.

After two years of my sponsorship it was time for her to find a local company that would offer an internship with the possibility of employment upon the completion of her degree.

Glendah's resourcefulness found SAFAIR, a South African air freight company and the person to plead her case to, Paul Van Wyk. I wrote a letter of recommendation for her focusing on her determination and work ethic. Mr. Van Wyk immediately responded to my letter. She was soon interviewed by a panel at SAFAIR and was able to answer each difficult question on airplane structure. They were impressed and early enrolled her in the Fall of 2004.

She was on her way to her dream.

In the meantime, Crystal came to live with her in the apartment we were providing for her. She met a policeman with whom she fell in love; they conceived a baby and she called to tell me she had "fallen pregnant" right in the middle of her final year of school.

Mr. Van Wyk and the faculty decided to hold her place in the class. Following the birth of little Tracy and further complications medically, she returned to school. She was burning the candle at both ends and the tension at home began to escalate.

Several middle-of-the-night calls from Johannesburg to New York would reveal that her man had turned violent, threatening to kill her and the girls. One bout landed her in the hospital with injuries from his hand. She had to be strong, get herself and the girls out of that environment and find help.

Glendah prevailed and made the moves she needed to make. A restraining order and a new girlfriend kept the man away.

As it turned out, the hydraulics work was more physically demanding on her petite body than it could endure. Her strength was in her character. She relinquished the position to the more hardy guys. She's currently in management and conducts expert training on the skin of the aircraft.

Her mother has moved to Johannesburg to live with and care for the girls while Glendah works to provide for her loved ones. She has her home, car and computer.

The girls are in school and have learned to speak English. Her mother is learning English, too. We're now connected through e-mail and Facebook.

Each time she questions me about how she could possibly repay me for what I've done for her, I simply implore, "Make sure your girls get their education." Pass it on.

On one visit to her home village, she was invited by her pastor one Sunday morning to tell her story of the American woman who said "yes" to her request. She simply encouraged the young people in the congregation to "keep praying, keep believing, keep your dream alive. And don't be afraid to ask. It can happen for you, too!"

There's no doubt in my mind that one day Glendah will make the long trip from South Africa to America and realize her dream of meeting Oprah.

Maybe she'll introduce me, too!

RECEIVE

When others offer to do an act of kindness for me, I'll allow myself *to* receive what it is they want to do.

It was a typical Southern California evening except for the fact that my parents were visiting from Ohio and I needed to run to the store to pick up our favorite evening snacks; popcorn, apples and Pepsi. It may not seem like the healthiest of munchies but in our home growing up it meant that we were all together sharing a television show, rooting for our favorite team event or playing a board game. I was thrilled to revisit those memories lodged in my taste buds.

I pulled up in the parking space at the closest convenience store near my home. Stepping from my car, I took a look at the dings and dents that had occurred in the five years since I'd driven it fresh and new off the lot. The damage was done in and around the Los Angeles airport, around the shopping malls and the office parking lot.

The radio was on the blink. The cruise control was no longer cruising. I was beginning to be ashamed of pulling up to any valet parking attendant because, as you may know in Los Angeles, you are what you drive.

Thinking to myself, "What am I doing driving this pile of junk? This car isn't worthy of me!" I saw him sitting with his back against the outside wall of the store and he was holding a money cup in his hand.

"Nice car you got there, lady."

"Nice car?" I reacted disbelieving what I had just heard. Then I found myself caught in a moment of gratitude. He was right. All in all, it was a nice car.

It was faithful to get me to and from my home to destinations on those unpredictable freeways surrounding Los Angeles; it was cool in the summer and warm in the winter; it was paid for in full which meant I had no monthly obligation except to keep the vitals checked and the tank filled.

I turned to this wise and generous man who sat begging for change and simply said, "Thanks, I do have a nice car." Additionally, I will offer assistance to someone. If they refuse my offer, I will gently ask them to pause, "replay" the scene, and allow themselves to accept my offer of help. This will help them breakthrough, too.

Asking and receiving. Two of the admonitions of the Master. And yet we are so reluctant to experience them. We must begin to allow others to do for us, and receive their gifts. Otherwise, we will die.

HOLD ONTO YOUR GOAL
DON'T LET GO OF YOUR DREAM
BEGIN TO BELIEVE THAT YOU ARE WHO YOU SEEM

EXPERIENCE THE MOMENT
TRUST THE HERE AND NOW
CHERISH ALL THE TIME SPENT

FOR IT TEACHES YOU SOMEHOW
TO
REACH FOR THE HIGHEST
ALLOW ONLY THE BEST
NEVER BE BIASED

MOVE AHEAD OF ALL THE REST
EXPRESS EVERY FEELING
SPEND SOME TIME ALONE

AND YOU'LL REALIZE THE BEAUTY OF
YOURSELF
YOUR FAMILY
YOUR HOME

16
FINANCES RADIATE
You Are A Star Right Where You Are

"Bring all the tithes into the storehouse so there will be enough food in my Temple. If you do, says the Lord Almighty, I will open the windows of Heaven. I will pour out a blessing so great you won't have enough room to take it in! Try it! Let me prove it to you!" Malachi 3:10

THE INTELLIGENT ONES ARE GENEROUS

This is the one scripture in the Bible where we read God actually prodding us to prove his promise. This promise is true, so what could possibly be stopping us from giving, trusting when I give the first 10% (yes that's ten percent) of my income to advancing spiritual good for others, my needs will be taken care of in abundant ways. Some say, "the truly intelligent ones are those who are generous."

Before I pay anyone else, I invest this as a statement of faith and loyalty to the One from whom I receive all creative, productive ideas - the ideas that turn into my income. I don't have to be afraid that that I'll run out. I'll always have enough to meet my needs.

The opportunity to join Mark Victor Hansen and Robert Allen and their band of Enlightened Millionaires, I learned a major life changing practice as it relates to tithing - or giving the first 10%.

In my life as a preacher's kid, I was exposed to faithful grandparents and parent who took the Lord at His word. They paid their tithe first, before anything else was paid. If creative financing needed to take place, 'robbing Peter to pay Paul' they would do that so that their tithe was never compromised.

For me, watching them take 10% and put it into the offering plate each week, I became fearful. If Daddy earned $100 from the church, and he gave back $10, that meant we had only $90 left.

I grew up living with the thought of 'lack' and what was 'left.'

That was until I learned from the Enlightened Millionaires. Their proposal was to encourage me to give 10% without fear of lack. Fear of not enough, the story I had told myself forever.

Earn 100%.
Give 10% in tithe.
And rather than it being a "subtractor" it becomes a "multiplier" so that you no longer live on what's left, 90% , but are abundantly blessed with 1000% to put toward good works, great experiences, expanded learning.

God doesn't know the meaning of poverty. When we're dealing with God's "prove me" promise, we're dealing with abundance.

When I read this for the first time I was stunned and filled with joy. No wonder our parents were confident and never can I recall an argument between them over finances. They dare not trust their meager income to anyone but the Lord and their faith in tithing.

To this day, the first check I write each month (yes, I still write checks), is my tithe check. The multiplier concept works! The 'return' on the tithe investment doesn't always come back in cash but can come back in a variety of ways.

From his book entitled <u>Quiet Moments with God</u>, Lloyd John Ogilvie, and Chaplain for the United States Senate asks these questions:

...Do I ever worry over money, having enough and keeping what I have?

...Is bill-paying time a stressful time for me?

...Has money ever been the focus of an argument or misunderstanding with people I love?

...Do I experience twinges of competition or envy over what others earn, have inherited or are able to do because of money?

...Do I ever spend money to solve hurt feelings, setbacks or disappointments?

...Do I worry excessively about inflation or what's happened to crack my nest egg?

...Do I tithe my income to glorify God and His work in the world?

The answers to these questions are the beginning of wisdom; when I get honest about the emotional hold money has on me, and admit exactly where I am financially, I can begin to get honest with all other relationships and situations in my life.

I'll commit to that kind of naked honesty beginning now.

What is the gross income printed on my paycheck? If don't receive a paycheck and are being paid in other forms, I calculate my gross monthly income is and write it in this space.

$_____

What is 10% of that number?

$_____

Remember, it's a multiplier! Not a subtractor!

Talk about an investment that's more sure and secure than anything Wall Street could promise. This is guaranteed. The equivalent may not come back to me directly in cash. It will come back in a variety of ways; in health, in ideas, in savings, in gifts. In being taken out for dinner, in being invited to stay in a friend's vacation home; I'll know when I'm being gifted for the gift I gave.

And the most important thing to remember when it's happening is to acknowledge where it's coming from (the real source), I accept it graciously, and am grateful.

INVESTING IN MY 'ME' FUND

Next, I acknowledge my worth and reward it.

I do this by setting an amount aside as a 'Me Fund.' It may be a savings account; it may be a private cash stash in a simple jar. How much I put into my 'Me Fund' may vary. As I become accustomed to doing it, I genuinely recognize my worth and reward myself.

I think of it as an evolution. At one time in my earning, I may have allowed myself to acquire only those things that I needed -- then I progressed to those things I wanted -- and now it's time to graduate to investing in those things I deserve.

The 'Me Fund' accumulates to provide me with purchasing power for some material goal, a meaningful experience, or help me achieve long-term security. This leads again to greater future giving power!

What is it I truly believe I deserve and am willing to have for myself?

MANAGING MY INCOME

My financial challenges may not result from inadequate income; they result from inadequate income **management.** When I learn to plan my earning, giving, investing and spending, I'll realize the financial goals I've set.

Accepting responsibility for learning how to meet my financial obligations plays the major role in taking care of others and myself. I answer the following questions honestly.

- ✓ Do I have a consistent plan for financial giving?
- ✓ Do I consider myself my best investment and have a 'Me Fund'?
- ✓ Do I have an adequate savings plan to cover my expenses should an emergency arise?

Do I use credit cards too frequently and increase the cost of my purchases by paying high interest rates?

Am I savvy in finding financial institutions that offer lower rates than I'm currently paying on those credit cards?

Before I can begin to plan for my financial future, I must understand where I am today. It's such a courageous feeling to "get naked" financially and truly admit what I earn, what I spend, what I charge, and what money "leaks" easily through my fingers.

As I allow myself to become vulnerable in the next experience, just remember to stay with it. Making me accountable in black and white and seeing where I am will put me well on my way to assuring my financial future.

I answer these basic questions and jot the answer next to each one.

What is my gross monthly income? $_____

I get paid in direct proportion to the value I bring to the market place. How much do I get to deliver to how many? How many do I want to affect?

What is my net monthly income? $_____

What are my monthly expenses?

Food $_____

Clothing $_____

House/Rent $_____

Insurance- $_____
    House/Car/Life/Health

Taxes $_____

Car Payment $_____

Car gas/oil/maintenance $_____

Phone $_____

Cable/Internet $_____

Utilities $_____

Credit Card(s) Payments $_____

Medical/Prescriptions $_____

Professional Services $_____

Recreation/Entertainment $_____

Other $_____

Monthly Expense Total $_____

What is my net income? $_____

$_____

Subtract the expenses from the net income.

$_____

If my bottom line is zero or minus, it's time to seriously take that first giant leap of faith and give 10% where it can bless and be blessed. It's the first sure step to financial discipline and balance.

I don't give because I *have* to; I give because I *get* to.

The return on my 10% may be in a variety of forms other than cash. However, as generosity is expressed to me, I'll begin to receive and recognize it as a 'gift' and I'll immediately be grateful. The more grateful I am, the more I'll have to be grateful for. The real deal is to be willing not to limit what I can gain, nor limit what I can lose.

All the money I'll ever earn comes through other people. Aligning my relationships is vital to my financial security.

Here's a story that demonstrates the point.

REDKEN Australia sponsored a great moment of growth for me. I was invited to train the Aussie sales and education team and to meet our leading salon professionals in the 'land down under'.

This dynamic team was brought together at the exclusive Opal Cove on the Eastern shore. Among the group were Bennie and Tracey Tognini of Brisbane.

One evening the Tognini's offered to give me a makeover. They arrived at my hotel room armed with all the tools of their trade that made them award-winning designers in hair and makeup.

As Bennie began cutting my hair, I said to Tracey, "I just wish I could get rich doing what I do." She looked around the beautifully appointed suite, through the plate glass windows overlooking the aquamarine water. Then she proceeded to teach me a lesson I'll never forget.

"Now, what would you do if you were rich?" she asked. "You'd travel around the world, stay in first class hotels and have people tending to your every need. Wake up, Ann. This is rich!" And so it was.

Yes, I've been blessed with being granted the opportunities of seeing places in the world I've ever wanted to see. Boarding airplanes in major cities, I look at the travel posters covering the walls of jet ways and say to myself as I pass them one-by-one, "I've been there, I've stayed there, I've eaten there." And I always remember to be thankful.

Traveling to my sister Jan's home for Thanksgiving one year, I noticed a bulletin board outside the United Methodist Church in the small Ohio town of Sunbury; I read the words, "A Grateful Mind is a Great Mind."

Great thought for Thanksgiving, great thought for today!

How about you?

Take a moment and define what "rich" is to you by using your five senses.

> *How does 'rich' look?*
> *How does 'rich' feel?*
> *How does 'rich' sound?*
> *How does 'rich' smell?*
> *How does 'rich' taste?*

From now on, I'll be aware of those 'rich' moments that provide me with the experiences to look, feel, sound, smell and taste what 'rich' is.

What I'll find is that I am rich already! And with my managed financial plan, my money will be there to verify it.

A lifelong friend, Paul Franklin, called one December to tell me he had been contemplating closing the doors of his film production business. He started his company over 25 years ago and had steady positive growth investing in people, equipment and locations.

Then with the unwise hiring of a new employee, he began to see the morale and competency of his business coming unraveled. He was at the brink when another employee recommended he read the now New York Times best seller, The Prayer of Jabez, written by Bruce Wilkinson.

Every day for thirty days, Paul made the Prayer his prayer. He prayed with sincerity, with humility. It was just a matter of time that the phones began ringing off the hook and business was - in his words - "coming out of the woodwork." He recommended that I read the book and begin practicing the same daily ritual.

In January I began. Day by day, I was faithful in my morning quiet time to repeat the prayer and affirm it as my truth. It was in the area of 'expanding my territory' that I began to see and feel the effects.

Modern Salon Magazine, the leading trade magazine in the U.S. asked that I write a bi-weekly column on their website entitled Spirit Moves; The American Beauty Association voted unanimously to appoint me as the chairperson for their annual charity ball; the president of the professional division of L'Oreal USA enlisted me to head a newsletter targeted to the 1000+ employees of the division.

These and many other 'territory expansion' opportunities have come my way, such as expanding the potential of my speaking opportunities in industries outside of the professional salon business. One of the most rewarding was SHAPE Magazine's Shape Your Life retreat - a series of long weekends dedicated to SHAPE readers who are ready to put action to their dreams and make the time and financial commitment necessary to change their body, minds, spirit.

For your own amazement, I'm including the prayer for you to begin today. It is written on a small card, which is in my daily meditation book so I remember to pray it. A friend of mine has his on his bathroom shelf, which reminds him to pray it as he shaves each morning. Copy it down, put it somewhere you'll see it daily, and watch the miracles begin to happen.

And Jabez called on the God Israel saying,
"Oh that You would bless me indeed, and enlarge my territory, that Your hand would be with me, and that You would keep me from evil that I may not cause pain."
So God granted him (or her) what he (or she) requested.
1 Chronicles 4:9-10

GOALS AND DREAMS AND PLANS AND SCHEMES
TRYING TO GET MY SHARE
OF LIFE AND LOVE
AND WEALTH
I SHOVE
AND IN SHOVING I GET NOWHERE
BUT IF I PAUSE AND JUST BE STILLED
I REALIZE MY DREAMS ARE BEING FULFILLED
SO I CAN REST IN PEACE
AND GIVE A SIGH OF RELEASE
FOR ALL MY HOPES AND DREAMS I FIND
ARE ALREADY MINE
THEY'RE ALREADY MINE
WHEN I'VE PICTURED THEM IN
MY MIND

PIANO AND VOCAL
GOALS AND DREAMS
ANN MINCEY
LIGHT WALTZ
WORDS AND MUSIC BY ANN MINCEY
INTRO
GOALS AND DREAMS PLANS AND SCHEMES TRYIN' TO GET MY SHARE.
OF LIFE, AND LOVE AND WEALTH I SHOVE AND IN SHOVING I GET NO WHERE...
BUT IF I PAUSE AND JUST BE, STILL I REALIZE MY DREAMS ARE BEING FUL-FILLED I'VE REST IN PEACE AND A SIGH OF RE-LIEF
MY HOPES AND DREAMS I FIND ARE AL READY MINE THEY'RE AL READY MINE

PIANO-VOCAL
ANN MINCEY
GOALS AND DREAMS
PAGE TWO
WHEN I PICTURE THEM IN MY
MIND
I'VE LIVED IN PEACE + GIVE A
SIGH OF RE- LIEF WHEN I PICTURE THEM IN MY
MIND MY MIND....
ritard
MUSIC PREPARATION:
BILL STEVENSON
SATURDAY AUGUST 29, 1998

17
SPIRIT RADIATES
You Are A Star Right Where You Are

"Do something beautiful for God and become beautiful doing it."
Psalm 90:17

This is the beginning and the end. Without God's Spirit - the source of loving kindness and passion, compassion and empathy, patience and surrender, none of the other points can or will radiate at their authentic brilliance.

This is the seat of acceptance of SELF in and others in this present moment.

We make time for the things that we value most. What would someone learn about me if they followed me around for three months? My values - not my habits - form the basis that becomes the routines of my life.

Housed here, too, are the two major life issues that can propel us to thrive.

They are forgiveness and gratitude.

FORGIVENESS IS EVERYTHING

The unforgiving attitude is about being stuck in the past. Past hurts, past betrayals, past disappointments; past mistakes, past misjudgments, past affairs; past...past...past...past...past.

Guess what! The past is passed. Don't go there.

Grief is housed in the past. And as long as I choose to dwell there, I'm not here. And if I'm not here, I'm grieving and missing what is happening, who is speaking, what feelings are aroused and what learning can be accomplished.

Grief is felt in the heart. The heart is affected. And it's no wonder why coronary disease is on the rise, since the heart muscle and the energy that feeds it trying to exist on the morsels that are thrown to it by the memories of what *was* rather than the fresh happenings of what *is*. Breast cancer - same energy center, same source, same effects.

Unrequited grief, leads to dis-ease and for many, death. And yet, even those that are alive are actually dead in the moment.

So to the point of forgiveness. I do it. Just do it. Do it now. Do it forever. I do it in the moment I feel the need to do it. I do it for what's been grieving me for years, months, days, and minutes. I write a "Dear Whomever" forgiveness letter to the one whom I believe I need to forgive, or whom I'd like to ask forgiveness. I don't have to send it.

It's not about them. It's about me and my willingness to ask or grant forgiveness. They never have to know I wrote it. But I do. And the minute I write it I'll feel the release of the load that it has kept me under. Like a runner trying to complete the New York Marathon with 10-pound sand bags on his/her legs, so does forgiveness bog me down with unnecessary burdens. I can run free.

This issue of being burdened reminds me of a traveling story. I was delivered to the American Airlines terminal at JFK airport in New York. Since I was going to be traveling for nearly three weeks to faraway places such as Seoul, Taiwan, Tokyo, Montreal and Nice, I loaded my three bags with everything I thought I would need for any situation in which I found myself.

Because of serious construction around the airport, it became apparent that I would roll my bags into the terminal and find an agent who could check me in. I must have been obviously weighed down and troubled when a skycap approached me with an empty luggage cart and a big smile. "Do you need some help?" he asked.

I looked at him as if to say, "Yeah, now you show up," because I had already made it through the construction maze to the inside where within a few steps I'd be at the Business Class check-in counter.

He gave me one more "Huh? May I help you?" I was still holding my heavy load feeling the pressure of the bags cutting through the handles of my bags to my palms.

"All you have to do is just say the word," he said. I said, "yes." He went into action. In a moment the load was lifted, I was all checked in.

This illustrates what the Spirit is saying to me everyday - "Just say the word and I'll take your load; your weights, your pain."

For me, sometimes, being stuck with the pain is more comfortable than the temporary pain of the 'shift' that would lead to pleasure.

The release of unnecessary weight is exactly what I believe happens when we forgive or ask for forgiveness. Sometimes all it takes is the willingness to write the note. It's serious stuff. You can do it.

Begin with the following:

Dear _____,

I forgive you completely for what you did to me. (Or) I want you to forgive me completely for what I did to you.

You can go into further detail if you need to purge deeply. Go ahead, Anguish, cry, get angry, stop writing, and start again. Whatever it takes. But write until your hand stops. You'll know you're finished. And you can begin to live.

It's no wonder Jesus admonished in The Lord's Prayer to 'forgive us our debts as we forgive our debtors' and the first words he spoke on the cross "Father, forgive them...."

He knew the physical, emotional and spiritual health - and yes, the eternal rewards that await - results from the act of forgiveness. Life begins with forgiveness.

According to an article in USA Today, August 28, 2001, studies at Stanford University reported by psychologist Carl Thoresen showed there is evidence of emotional and physical health payoffs from the act of forgiveness. "Those who learned to forgive also saw stress, anger and psychosomatic symptoms - headaches, stomach upsets, etc. - go way down significantly lower than for the control group."

After forgiveness comes gratitude. Life thrives on gratitude.

HOW CAN I SAY THANKS

You read about being grateful for the gifts that come as the results of giving. We spoke of being grateful for people and telling them so. Now it's time to express your gratitude. Remember, "I only have what I express."

Just as we wrote a letter of forgiveness, let's now compose a letter of thankfulness to someone who means so much to you. Someone who has been there for you. Someone who has gone to bat for you or been your advocate. Someone who's never passed judgment, been critical. Or someone who for the benefit of your own good was willing to take the risk and give you honest feedback.

You know who it is. This letter you may want to send. Or this call you may want to make. It will fill your heart and theirs. A bond will be set for life. You'll be able to count on each other even more deeply than before.

Again, simply put your pen on the page and just begin to write.

Dear _____,

How can I say thanks for the things that you've done for me.

And then go into specifics on those memories or issues where you felt the supportive, guiding hand of your friend. It doesn't have to be long; it just has to be heartfelt. And they will feel you through the words on the page. Just as you would like to hear from someone you've done something special for, write to your special someone in the same tone, words and feelings.

They'll get it. And they'll never be the same.

Earlier, we suggested the deep breathing exercise using the words "Breathe in Joy, Breathe out Fear."

Now, I want you to have another sensation. Sit with your back pressed against the chair; relax your shoulders and face. Close your eyes. Take three cleansing breaths in through the heart and out through the solar plexus with these words:

- ❖ *"Breathe in Gratitude, Breathe out Forgiveness."*
- ❖ *"Breathe in Gratitude, Breathe out Forgiveness."*
- ❖ *"Breathe in Gratitude, Breathe out Forgiveness."*

Check in with your body, mind, emotions, spirit.... how do you feel? Sit in this feeling until you absolutely have to move.

HeartMath, a highly researched scientific approach to stress management and creativity, was introduced to me at the 2003 Spirit in Business conference in San Francisco.

The originators of HeartMath showed quantitative results on the reduction of stress hormones by two predominant actions; Heart Lock-in and Freeze Frame.

Write in your journal the 10 things you have to be grateful for this moment. At the end of the day, ask yourself this question, "When were the times today when I felt grateful?".

I WILL RE-CHOICE AND BE GLAD

One Sunday morning I was watching the Hour of Power broadcast from the Crystal Cathedral in Garden Grove, California. On many working Sundays I've turned on my television in the hotel room and while getting ready for a seminar or training session I've worshipped in the beauty of the palm trees swaying in the backdrop of that architectural wonder of the world.

I've been there. I've heard the mighty pipe organ accompanying the choir's voices singing, "Morning has broken, like the first morning, blackbird has spoken like the first bird..." From my hotel room, I projected myself into the pew and looked into the eyes of the pastor as he greeted me.

Dr. Robert Schuller rose to the pulpit in his robe and colorful doctoral shawl to call us to worship.

His familiar imploring words rang through that massive, glass-enclosed building, "This is the day the Lord has made. Let us rejoice and be glad in it."

If you've ever heard the exuberance of Dr. Schuller's voice and his distinct pronunciations, you'll understand when I tell you I heard something new when he called me to worship that day.

What I heard was, "This is the day the Lord has made. Let us **re-choice** and be glad in it."

"Re-choice." That's what it's all about.

Daily I have the ability and opportunity to re-choose the way that I live, the ways I give, the things I say. Just as the words across the bottom of the window shades at SAKS Fifth Avenue remind me that the artisans are changing the mood and fashions on the mannequins inside and their work is indeed a WORK IN PROGRESS, so is my life.

And the choices I make moment by moment, day by day are creating the artwork that I'm putting my signature on for the world to see.

I don't let my past dictate who I am, but I let it be a part of who I will become. Dream large, pray large, receive large.

I can imagine God saying to us, "I have no one except you to help me to realize your dream." This excites me to respond to God and say, "Yes!"

Ninety percent of life is showing up. I don't know what's going to happen, but I know nothing's going to happen if I don't show up.

With every breath I take, I have a choice to make.

IN THE MORNING ALL I HEAR ARE THE BIRDS AND YOUR VOICE

ANOTHER DAY THAT YOU HAVE MADE

ANOTHER CHANCE TO RE-CHOICE

RE-CHOICE IN THE WAYS THAT I LIVE
RE-CHOICE IN THE WAYS I CAN GIVE
RE-CHOICE EVERYTHING THAT I SAY
DAY
AFTER
DAY
AFTER
DAY
I HAVE THE CHOICE.

ANY WONDER I AWAKE WITH A 'YES' ON MY MIND
'YES' TO LOVING

ONE ANOTHER

AND 'YES' TO BE KIND

RE-CHOICE IN THE WAY THAT I LIVE
RE-CHOICE IN THE WAYS I CAN GIVE
RE-CHOICE EVERYTHING THAT I SAY
DAY
AFTER
DAY
AFTER
DAY
I HAVE THE CHOICE

Anything that makes me feel less than joyful is not coming from Love. I can, in the instant, make the choice to separate myself from anything that separates me from Love.

LOVING SERVICE IS A GENTLE THING

The salon environment with its transformers of beauty that listen with a caring ear and compassionate touch, is one of the last safe places on earth where Love is spoken and demonstrated. It is an atmosphere where miracles take place.

From the birth of a baby and his first haircut, through the first day of school, high school proms, college graduations and weddings; divorces, career transfers and saying goodbye in death, the salon professional plays a vital role in every life stage for her clients. No one else, except perhaps a church congregation, has the intimate knowledge of families and their life triumphs and traumas as the salon professional.

And so, in this atmosphere of Love, a client can feel safe to share highs, lows, sorrows, joys, achievements, failures, disappointments, losses and gains. To tell their innermost secrets and be held in the process takes a special person in a special place. Love is a kingdom where things are turned upside down.

As a familiar phrase from the 12-step program reminds us, 'we are only as sick as our secrets.' When a salon client feels safe to tell their innermost secrets, be gently touched in the process, and leave the experience looking more beautiful or handsome, they are not as sick as they were when they arrived. They have been healed.

I'm reminded of Dr. Ron DiSalvo, REDKEN's vice president of research and development on a seminar platform in 1975. It was my first educational event as a new field representative. Ron was facing the group with his finger pointing out towards the future when he said, "In the 1990's hairdressers will be the doctors of the future."

"The 1990's," I thought, "that's eons away." And yet, here we are in the new millennium and Ron was right. The Latin word for "Doctor" is translated "Teacher." Certainly the salon professionals I've been privileged to know are teaching their clients about themselves in ways beyond the common haircut or hair color design.

Salon professionals including hair designers, hair colorists, nail technicians, estheticians and massage therapists are offering healing touch and healing conversation with every person who steps into their healing environment.

These 'doctors' connect with people, interacting at their most vulnerable place, offer treatments and offer hope and counsel. They increase health by improving the quality of the client/guests' life.

I've seen with my own eyes, when salon professionals are willing to surrender their talents and gifts to God they begin to see their "job" turn into their "work."

It becomes their mission to contribute to the spirit and the image of their clients. They rest in the knowledge they'll be rewarded spiritually with Love that is never-ending and forever refreshing. As Saint Francis of Assisi prayed..."For it is in giving, that we receive."

People will clamor to the doors of those salons filled with balanced "Star Servers" to feel enclosed within their safe harbor.

Today, more than ever, the salon will be needed for these purposes.

WILLING TO BE A SERVANT

Now we can proceed to do the work of healing gently through serving humbly by glowing brightly. To begin the process, I want to focus on willingness to serve.

I didn't say be a slave, I said to serve.

The privilege of serving is acknowledged in ancient scriptures as the first honor..."we must be the servants of all." Even the Master humbled himself to wash the feet of his friends. When the macho disciple Peter refused and declared, "You're not washing my feet!" Jesus replied, "If you don't allow me to wash your feet, you're not one of me."

Peter relented. "All right, my hands and my head as well."

At that moment, Jesus set up the first model of a full service salon and the full service servant.

If that work was something he did to prove humility and generosity it's certainly a great endorsement of what happens every day in salons worldwide.

Service is the idea
"Serve Us" is the action

To thrive in your service is a result of aligning your star's five points of freedom.

Being **willing to serve** is an issue of the **spirit and of clear and clean thoughts**
Being **able to serve** your pure relationships the privilege of the **bright body**
which will result in
Being **rewarded** with **bountiful resources.**

Take a few minutes to ponder this thought.

ABUNDANCE FOLLOWS MY CAPACITY TO SERVE

Now answer these questions.

"How abundant do I want to be?"
"How fully can I serve?"
"How fully can I be present to find a need and serve it?"

I invite you to join me as we look up into the night skies we think of those who have gone before us as the brilliant stars.

Can we be bold and courageous to proclaim our own shine here on earth? Will you join me in doing whatever it takes to 'shine out like the stars holding out the word of life' to all who come into your world?

Take a long look at the star field on the American flag and claim one of those stars as your very own. Every time you see the flag from now on, reaffirm your place as that star by saying "That's me!" Commit to the healthy awareness of the five points we've covered in this book.

It is my conviction that America will stay beautiful as Americans stay beautiful and healthy, positive and financially sound, and as they serve from a heart of love.

We are blessed to be in a country where we have the freedom to be beautiful.

As we've seen the pictures of women covered from head to toe and then compare those images with women I see on the streets of New York everyday - carrying their iPhones which gives them the knowledge of the world, in any language, anywhere on the planet in the palm of their hands, catching a bus ride, hailing a taxi, wearing whatever they want to wear…. I give thanks for a country where we have the freedom to "Be You to Full."

I give thanks for living in a country where we have the freedom to create the beauty of peace and the peace of beauty. The industry I serve dedicates itself to this as they turn the key to their salons' doors every single day.

And I give thanks for living in a country where I've had the freedom to encourage each other to learn the best techniques and technologies; to earn the highest income; to live the best life they can dream of.

I'm thankful that my company, REDKEN, has dedicated its educational mission for over five decades to the opportunity for every salon professional in the world to be Learning, Earning and Living Better.

As we celebrate these freedoms let's dedicate ourselves to them in honor of those who no longer have the opportunity to enjoy the pursuit of beauty.

18
RESONATE
You Are A True Work Of Heart

"When wisdom entereth into thine heart and knowledge is pleasant to thy soul; discretion shall preserve thee, understanding shall keep thee." Proverbs 2:10-11

Empowered by the vision of my dad and mother sitting at their breakfast table praying for me, the scriptures that were brought to bring me the spiritual direction of my life, and the life-giving truth of being a star as I held out word of life, I was now fortified for the unfathomable unfolding of events including a corporate acquisition of REDKEN by L'Oreal USA, the Northridge earthquake, relocation from California to New York City, eye-witnessing the attack on the World Trade Center, an early retirement from REDKEN and an unexpected journey of faith and love.

I would've never dreamed in a million years that I'd live in New York City and have a love affair with it.

I'd travel to New York City on business trips, normally once a year for the huge International Beauty Show at the Javits Center. After about three days my skin would begin to crawl and I'd speak under my breath, "get me out of here!" California's sunny days and palm trees were always a welcome sight when I'd return home.

It was in April of 1993 when Paula called us into her office to announce we would be meeting with a management group from Cosmair, New York. We were to prepare presentations of our various departments, projects and projections.

Without hesitation we went into action and within days found ourselves sitting around a large oak table in the conference room of the Marriott Hotel in Woodland Hills, CA. The visitors from the east entered the room, we welcomed them and the business of the day began.

Within two months, June 21, 1993, to be exact, all employees gathered in the ballroom of the same Marriott and with music playing and big screen ablaze with the REDKEN logo, we were in for an announcement that would change our world forever.

Paula approached the podium and began. She was gracious as she read from a script that included a mission statement which we believed was REDKEN's...scientific approach, worldwide expansion, education for every salon professional.

"Whose mission statement is this?" Paula asked. We answered, "It's our mission statement," to which she replied, "Oh, it sounds very much like our mission, but it's actually taken from L'Oreal Professional. And it's because of the alignment of our two companies' mission, I'm announcing today that REDKEN will be acquired by L'Oreal."

Employees, who looked at their work as their life and dedicated themselves totally to it, sat stunned at her announcement. We had, up to that point, stood on platforms imploring the salon stylists to keep the business of beauty in the salon, especially when it came to permanent waves and hair color.

And now our parent company was the largest beauty company in the world doing business through mass, luxury and professional markets.

An immediate dilemma, but we trusted Paula and her "road signs" to consider acquisition that had come since John had suffered a heart attack and had to scale back from his leadership as president.

She had borrowed $58 million in 1988 to buy back the outstanding public stock with the promise to pay it back in five years.

The announcement of acquisition came in 1993, five years later. She was prepared both professionally and personally.

An interesting lead up to this "corporate courtship" and ultimate consummation was something I personally was involved in and one of the highlights of my life with REDKEN.

Every four years the World Championships of Hairdressing was celebrated, much like the Olympics are for athletes. On a rotation, the United States was to be the host country for the event in 1984 and Paula was determined to put REDKEN on the global map.

Designed by Tom Saponaro, our exhibit space was the never-before-experience we called "Walk Through the Hair Shaft" a literal Disney-type, full-sensory three minutes of "Beauty Through Science".

When the international guest would enter the enclosed 'tunnel' they would walk on foam flooring which simulated the scalp. On the walls photos of damaged hair were projected showing the effects of harsh chemicals in most permanent wave solutions, which now would be combined with the scent of burning hair, wafting through the air.

As the guest walked closer to the exit there would be the sound of a solution added to the hair, photos of healthy hair projected and strains of the Hallelujah Chorus sounded in declaration of the reconstruction of the damaged hair by REDKEN's hydrolyzed protein product, PPT-S77. Hallelujah!!!

Thousands of visitors walked through during the three-day event and REDKEN was on everybody's lips….and hair, as they were all given samples of the products upon exiting. Genius.

Another genius idea came from Paula and was my task to complete prior to the guests' arrival.

She had read an article about taxi drivers in San Francisco who earned higher tips when their cabs were clean, smelled fresh AND if they were well-groomed.

Her assignment for me was to travel to Las Vegas where Hair World was to be hosted, convince the taxi cab companies' principles that it would be a good thing to have REDKEN groom their drivers prior to the salon world's invasion of their city. They agreed and we set a date for the drivers to come to the Hilton Hotel for complimentary haircuts done by a staff of REDKEN stylists.

The drivers walked away from their grooming experience with two small bags; one filled with REDKEN/RK products for their personal use and one filled with small, red ceramic heart-shaped pins with the sentiment "REDKEN LOVES ME."

The only request we made was for the drivers to give them to anyone who rides in their cab during Hair World.

One of those international visitors was Alain Leprince-Ringuet, the vice president of L'Oreal Professional Products Division in Paris. He arrived into Las Vegas' McCarran Airport, found his way to a taxi and asked to be driven to the Hilton Hotel.

When he was delivered to the hotel, he reached over the front seat to pay his fare and in exchange he received a "REDKEN LOVES ME" heart pin.

When Alain told this story to me he said, "I looked at that heart in the palm of my hand and said, Paula Kent is in town."

From that moment, L'Oreal began and continued for nine years to "corporately court" Paula.

It's amazing what a little heart can do!

After REDKEN's acquisition in June 1993, it was explained and we understood that we would continue our operation on the West Coast. We were introduced to a new General Manager and we'd have all the resources of L'Oreal USA in New York. All was well.

Daddy and Mother came to Los Angeles for a post-Christmas visit. We drove to Pasadena to witness the building of the Rose Parade floats and returned the next morning to "oohh and ahhh" as the floats made their way down the parade route, Sitting on bleachers in the freezing pre-dawn hours, drinking hot chocolate and cuddling together under blankets, these were memories that would be forever imprinted in my mind.

On Sunday we agreed we'd veer away from attending a Nazarene church and make our way to Hollywood Presbyterian Church where Lloyd John Ogilvie was the pastor. With the 'voice of God,' Dr. Ogilvie presented a vital New Year's message. At the conclusion he invited the congregation to come forward to pray with him or one of the church deacons in dedication to the Lord for the New Year.

I went forward, waited until Dr. Ogilvie was available and walked to him. He said, "How can I pray for you?"

"I need a new idea," were my only words in response.

Dr. Ogilvie placed his hands on my shoulders and began to pray. At the conclusion of the prayer he looked into my eyes, smiled as he pointed Heaven-ward and said, "It's on its way!"

After my folks departed for Ohio the following Sunday, that night January 16th, I was sitting in the safety of my new condominium that I'd just moved into and finished decorating over the Christmas holidays.

Sipping tea, watching the fire in the fireplace, listening to smooth jazz on my sound system, I was so grateful and began thanking God out loud for my beautiful safe harbor.

At around eleven o'clock, I prepared my home for the night, made my way up the stairs to my master bedroom and fell into a gentle sleep.

At four-thirty in the morning, I was shot from my bed. The whole house was swinging, shaking. I made my way over to the doorjamb with outstretched arms holding on and stood there swaying and listening to my house breaking apart downstairs.

I was confident I knew what it was.... the Big One...the earthquake we'd been warned about and unconsciously waiting for. Without thought, I began singing at the top of my lungs an old hymn of the church:

> ***"On Christ the solid rock I stand***
> ***All other ground is sinking sand***
> ***All other ground is sinking sand"***
> Edward Mote

No one can lay any foundation other than the one already laid, which is Jesus Christ. I Corinthians 3:11

Oh how happy I was that my first response was not of anger or fear, it was a response of faith and hope. Singing one of the old hymns of the church gave me calm.

Finally, after 48 seconds, the movement stopped. I pulled on some warm clothes and shoes and made my way outside to the parking lot where I huddled with my neighbors. Pre-dawn, January in California it was cold.

The pastor of a small Church of the Nazarene walked across the street and offered us to come to safety provided by the strength of his A-frame constructed sanctuary. There we were served coffee, donuts and given blankets to stay warm in the early hours of morning.

When the sun began to break, I walked through the church and saw a telephone. Never dreaming there would be a clear line, I jokingly picked it up...and voila! There was a dial tone.

My parents - always my first point of contact - was the first call I wanted to make. They had been watching Good Morning America and saw the destruction. How relieved they were to know I was all right. I remember speaking through my tears something about "learning the lesson of 'just things' and would call them again soon to keep them informed of what I discovered when I re-entered my home."

It was shocking the first glimpse of my safe harbor. The peaceful place of just a few hours before was now in shambles. Daddy had helped me build a wall of bookshelves in the living room to house my friends, my books and the treasures I'd collected from around the world.

The bookcases and fireplace bricks had fallen, the glass top tables broken, the kitchen cabinets and refrigerator jarred open, glass and food everywhere.

I slowly made my way through the rubble with yet another song running through my head.

> *"Where the Spirit of the Lord is, there is peace*
> *Where the Spirit of the Lord is, there is love*
> *There is comfort in life's darkest hour*
> *There is light and life there is hope and power*
> *In the Spirit, in the Spirit of the Lord"*
> Steve Adams

Where the Spirit of the Lord is, there is freedom. 2 Corinthians 3:17

I tried to think of where to begin the clean up process. I made my way upstairs to my bedroom and bathroom. I saw the same scene. Water everywhere.

I pulled the shower curtain back and there were my REDKEN products. They must have moved with every jolt until they stopped - plastic containers huddled together at the drain.

When I looked at them, my imagination heard them say, "Don't worry Annie, we're still here."

I smiled.

My angel friend and colleague, Anita Schertzer, offered her home, located high on a solid rock that did not move in the earthquake, and I moved in for the days that it took for me to reestablish my living space.

After all these years, I'm forever grateful to Anita for her generosity and soothing care.

In the ensuing days and weeks, we repaired our company, our homes and our lives. We were a short five miles from the epicenter of the 6.8 quake and had a real jolt.

The biggest after-shock was still to come.

Within days, our general manager gathered the education department together to discuss our upcoming International Seminar scheduled for three weeks out. It was incredulous to think that those of us who didn't have even a functional toilet in our homes would be in the mindset to plan a seminar for 700 guests.

We were galvanized to move forward and we did. Somehow, with Divine intervention, we produced the seminar at which the Cosmair (L'Oreal USA) management was in attendance.

This was the first time they 'felt and saw' REDKEN in action with our loyal salon customers and distributors from around the world. They came away with one overriding impression expressed by our CEO and President, Guy Peyrelongue.

"REDKEN is not in a building, REDKEN is in the hearts of these people, so you can take the people, put them anywhere and you'll still have REDKEN."

It was announced that REDKEN would move to New York City, the headquarters of L'Oreal USA and all those invited to make the move would be relocated by Labor Day, September, 1994.

"New York, oh no! Not New York!" was my first reaction. There was nowhere on the planet I wanted to live less than in New York. Ugly and loud, rude and big, boisterous and dirty New York.

Say it isn't so!

But it was so. And when all was said and done thirty-thee of us - out of 300 employees - said "We'll go" and by the Fall, we were "New Yorkas."

My decision to go wasn't that easy. It wasn't a done deal right off the bat. It wasn't until Easter Sunday evening that I had an affirmation that I needed to be a part of the group who would make the move.

After attending Easter morning service celebrating at Hollywood Presbyterian Church, I sat at my pool that afternoon, sunshine warming my body and melting my thoughts. In about an hour, my normal sunning time, I "heard" the Lord say "Go into your house and watch Beauty and the Beast," my favorite animated film of all time.

I obeyed. I popped a big bowl of popcorn, sat in front of my TV, pushed 'play' and began watching the story of Belle, and the ugly, loud, rude, big and boisterous, dirty Beast. I watched the story closely looking for the message I was bound to receive.

I began to relate to Belle. Frail scared and threatened (acquisition, earthquake, move) and there was the Beast, (New York.... oh my goodness it was the same!) I continued watching.

Something began to happen to Belle as she was exposed in a variety of situations with the Beast. She recognized redeeming qualities like playfulness, compassion, and generosity. His sharing the moment in the library was the best example of finding out what others want and "giving them what they want" ~ my dad's favorite five words of success.

It wasn't until Belle was willing to be the first to say "I Love You" that the Beast transformed.

There it was! My answer whether to go to New York City or not. I changed my perspective of New York and decided to be the first to say "I Love You New York." From the moment I arrived I saw the beauty, playfulness, compassion and generosity of New Yorkers.

It was going to be just fine.

More importantly, for our customers, there was a continuity of business with those of us Californians who knew them by name and wanted them to feel secure in the major changes that were impending.

And it has been just fine. For seventeen years, I found myself defending the redeeming qualities of my home and wanting to do whatever I could do to restore the hopes and dreams of New York and New Yorkers, of America and Americans. I know it's through demonstrating Love in all that I think, say and do - because Love and Fear cannot dwell in the same space at the same time.

I choose love. I choose to serve. I choose to radiate as the star that I am. Will you join me?

You will find, as I have, the more authentic we live, the more we are trusted. Others will sense how congruent we are- all radiating points aligned. What they're drawn to is not *me* as much as it is their own radiance - their own faith -they sense in us.

This is the happily ever after.

I was invited to spend a few moments one evening with a visiting Japanese priest who was taking private sessions with individuals on fifteen-minute segments. I made an appointment, showing up ten minutes ahead of my appointment time.

After waiting a few minutes a young Japanese boy came to escort me into a counseling room. He asked if I had three issues that I wanted to discuss with the monk - relating to health, job, family, relationship. I thought for a moment, and then responded. "I don't think I have three issues. But, if I did, they would be (1) I want to know I'm living from my authentic energy; (2) I want my body to reflect that authentic energy and need to know how to feed it, rest it exercise it; (3) I want to speak with boldness from that authentic energy. The boy wrote the three issues in Japanese on a three by five card and thanked me - after looking at me strangely and admitting that these were different requests than what they normally hear.

The boy escorted me back to the living room. Shortly a Japanese girl came to take me in to see the monk. Dressed in traditional robes, with a slick-bald head and small wire-rimmed glasses, he sat on a chair in the corner of the room.

I sat in front of him on the floor comfortable on a pillow. The girl took her place to my left. She handed him my card. He looked at it, read it thoroughly, and began laughing, his voice resonating and filling the entire room with its richness.

My little Annie took her first shot in my head. "Oh no, I'm so stupid. What did I say that was so funny? How is he going to respond to Me?"

Then he spoke and through her came the translation.

"What are you afraid of?"

I actually began to answer him with the first word that came to my mind, "Power."

But before I could speak he continued.

"You were born with this. Believe God 100% and that is all."

Looking at the girl, I said, "That's all?" And she nodded. I asked if I could touch him and just as I said it, he reached out his hands and I placed each one on the sides of my face. I gave her a hug. I left the room.

Some people felt healed following their session. Some felt definite energy shifts. I felt nothing. Just a nice experience that I probably wouldn't have again. But I couldn't get his words out of my mind and heart….Believe God 100% and that is all.

19
The Transition Of REDKEN
From California To New York

In the transition of REDKEN from California following the acquisition by L'Oreal USA to New York in 1994, I was approached to accept a new role as Director of Public Relations.

I knew nothing about PR, especially in the publishing and media capitol of the world. A daunting task as this position offered many new opportunities to meet and present REDKEN to the beauty editors of the major fashion and beauty magazines, trade publications and media.

I sure didn't want the fact that I had zero experience in classic PR to blow it or embarrass the company.

L'Oreal was gracious to move us into a suite of offices in the 575 Fifth Avenue location putting us right in the heart of the City. With our sister companies who were already friendly with the press through advertising and public relations, we were literally handed our professional goal by our general manager on a silver platter.

That goal was to achieve the number one position in press mentions ahead of all our professional beauty industry competitors. A huge goal. The question was not "could we" but rather "how will we?"

My first move was to hire well. And I did. Suzanne Brewer, smart, lovely, energetic

With the abundant talent pool within the L'Oreal world, I interviewed an assistant recommended from the fragrance division for our position of manager, public relations.

Suz walked into the interview with an immaculate resume and a 'look book' of events and releases she had been a part of planning and executing. I proceeded to walk her through the interview process and was just about to thank her for her time when she sat up on the edge of her chair.

With directness I hadn't seen in other candidates, Suz leaned in, looked at me with her piercing blue eyes and said, "I can do this job."

I was impressed. I knew she could do this job. I thanked her for her time and presentation. She left the office and I continued to interview eleven remaining candidates with various levels of education and experience.

I couldn't get the image of Suzanne Brewer out of my head.

Taking a break at lunch, I walked to the elevator bank to get some lunch and bring it back to my desk to devour before calling in the next candidate.

The elevator doors opened and out stepped Suzanne, taking me by surprise. "Thank you again for your time," she said, to which I blurted out, "I will see you later." In that moment, I confirmed my decision. She would be our manager.

With Suzanne in place we now needed a department assistant. A pile of resumes arrived and with them, again, the best suited candidate presented herself.

Kristen Kramer, a beauty with fashion model physique and bright mind, was our first choice. The serendipity of Kristen's hiring was just too good not to include here. She had been upstate in Poughkeepsie visiting family and waiting on the train platform. She would be hard to miss with her unique short, short, short haircut and height.

Suz was on the train and, looking out the window, she definitely noticed.

Within days, that same young women, Kristen Kramer, walked into our office to interview for our assistant carrying her PR credentials from Hofstra University. Suz couldn't believe her eyes. She and Kristen would be working closely so I fully agreed with Suz when she expressed her choice.

It was this combination of Suzanne's L'Oreal experience coupled with Kristen's perspective and my REDKEN tenure that made for a perfect storm to achieve our goals.

Our interpretation of PR was simply, "personal relationships" which manifested by developing friendships with beauty editors and media producers. We learned the secret of inclusion, making a connection with the editors' assistants and always including them in our gifting of new product offerings or Christmas presents….and everything in between.

We also recognized when the editor was getting married, or having a baby, REDKEN PR was generous to send a gift, a card, something to let them know they were important to us off the page, too.

Through these relationships we influenced millions of consumers to visit REDKEN salons for services and products. Recognition of REDKEN in the mind of the consumer was growing. In the beginning of our quest it would be rare that when I replied to a conversation, "What do you do?"

I replied, "I'm Director of Public Relations at REDKEN."

"REDKEN?" Do you mean Revlon? What is REDKEN?"

It was so gratifying as we continued to execute our department goals that the name REDKEN became a household word.

Through REDKEN public relations the company has provided teams of salon professionals behind the scenes of the major runways of New York, London, Paris and Milan Fashion Weeks led by session artist Guido Palau, named by Women's Wear Daily as one of 50 "Power Players" shaping the beauty industry.

We must note, however, that we didn't just jump into the major fashion scene in one fell swoop. It took years to develop the hairstyling teams and establish the budgets to be a player on these platforms. The truth is that we started with our then artistic directors Philip and Mary Wilson creating hair designs on the models of the senior students at Parsons School of Design.

We always want to recall and be grateful for how far we've come.

In December 1996, because of the work ethic, their sense of urgency, the creativity and the artistic tastes of both Suz and Kristen, I was named Vice President, Public Relations.

In the restructuring of REDKEN'S global education and marketing teams, general manager, REDKEN Worldwide, Michael Tanguy expanded the my title to Vice President, Global Education Development and Communications in June, 1998. Our focus was targeted to the development of trainers and public relations worldwide. Accomplishing our goals, in April 1999 I was named Vice President, Global Communications.

Within this alignment, global communications sent consistent REDKEN messages to the public relations managers in the international countries. Our major message, "At REDKEN, we have supreme respect for all salon professionals." Every contact we made with the press and media was to emphasize the necessity of the salon as a 'retreat' for consumers worldwide and the use of REDKEN products to recreate the salon experience at home in between salon visits.

REDKEN'S move to New York opened many doors that have contributed to updating our image - while maintaining our scientific heritage. We observed and asked "What's happening on the street?" then developed products that created the season's looks while keeping the hair in supremely healthy condition. We always said, "Great stuff happens when science leaves the labs and hits the streets." The reputation of "The Scientific Approach to Hairdressing" and "Beauty Through Science" lived on.

With a solid and powerful public relations team in place, I was focused on expanding REDKEN's influence and culture throughout the professional industry domestically and internationally. Invitations came to travel to each state in the United States, every Providence of Canada, and on to the five major continents, 28 countries in all. Invitations came from outside the industry as well. To my amazement, these personal contacts resulted in recognition, honors and awards beyond my wildest expectations.

1999 Southern Nazarene University celebrated its 100th Anniversary by naming 100 outstanding alumni to receive the Century Medallion in honor of their contribution to their specific areas of service. My Alma Mater counted me as one of the recipients for World Impact on Business by serving salon professionals on five continents.

2002 The American Beauty Association's honorary chairperson for the Annual Beauty Ball and Charity Auction scheduled in New York Times Square's Marriott Marquis "American Beauty...A Work of Heart" and surrounding cause marketing benefited The American Heart Association in the amount of $572,050. The reason for this charity for the beauty industry was obvious. Heart disease and stroke is the primary causes of death among American women. "Our industry is female-populated and the information on research and prevention is vital to our customers."

2002 "The Beauty of Peace and the Peace of Beauty" to a prestigious group of women executives, religious and spiritual leaders in Geneva Switzerland. 700 women attended The Women's Global Peace Initiative from 75 countries that came together under the sponsorship in part by the United Nations, to speak one word, 'Peace.'

2002 honored by the New York Women's Agenda, an organization of 100 women's groups representing 100,000 women in the greater New York City area, one of six women receiving the "STAR" Award as a tribute to her achievements which have inspired others to stretch themselves, by mentoring and advancing women, developing a new generation of leaders in various fields.

2003 the Annual North American Hairstyling Awards, January, was inducted into NAHA'S Hall of Leaders. This award highlighted my contributions to the salon industry through education of salon professionals worldwide and consumers through speaking and training and the printed word online for Modern Salon.com and Hair Color and Design Magazine.

2004 The City of Hope bestowed its prestigious Spirit of Life award at a gala event in conjunction with Cosmoprof in Las Vegas and named the

2004 honoree accepting the award on behalf of those in my family and at REDKEN who've suffered the trauma of breast and other life-threatening diseases. To celebrate the research and health of women worldwide based on the dedication of the doctors and researchers at City of Hope, I led the industry in raising a record-making $1,400,000.

2004 Inducted into The National Cosmetologist Association Hall of Renown honoring for contributions to the association.

2007 Intercoiffure of North America Inspiration Award recognizing outstanding service to the professional beauty industry, "helping salon professionals achieve their full potential both as cosmetologists and as persons. She inspires not only with her message but also by her example," said Lois Christie, the president of Intercoiffure America/Canada.

2007 Canadian Hairdresser Magazine "Mirror Award" Lifetime Achievement in serving salon professionals from Newfoundland to British Columbia.

2010 Raylon Corporation's "Art of Business" award bestowed each year to a special individual who has made an 'over and above' contribution to the business side of the salon industry.

2010 Professional Beauty Associations "Legends" award honoring a lifetime career of motivating, inspiring and supporting countless salon professionals, distributors and salon clients, and having been honored by every major industry organization and association.

2010 HeartMath "Lives Touched" Award for the 2,500 salon professionals who were trained in living a coherent life through the techniques and technologies of HeartMath.

2013 at the Waldorf-Astoria in New York City where the Intercoiffure of North America and Canada presented the Paula Kent Meehan "Light the Way" award in honor of the Founder of REDKEN Laboratories.

I've never created a company, developed a product or marketing program, I've never led a major team or been at the helm to take the credit or the failures of a business plan. When my colleagues were diligently staying at home and keeping the company running, I was known as "the woman who traveled around and blew sunshine."

Truly, all I ever did in retrospect was to listen and love. **Listen** and **Love**.

Initiating conversations that revolved around "everyday I'm in the office is one more day I'm not out with our customers, doing what I do best," generated the move for our PR department to the marketing umbrella.

Kristen's marriage to paparazzi photographer Charles Sykes (whose foot she stepped on at a concert at the Roseland Ballroom, got his attention and they fell in love), her subsequent decision to stay home with their first baby boy was followed by Suzanne and her husband John making the decision to move to Maine to raise their son.

One great decision in those days of transition was the hiring of a brilliant university graduate, her name, Darienne Weppler. With her seemingly shy ways, Darienne was a 'secret weapon' while she was learning and absorbing the world of professional beauty, she was observing the way of the future and began to take her own leadership position in the company.

Today, Darienne is the Vice President of Integrated Marketing Communications for REDKEN and Pureology. She's a shining star, carrying herself and our brand with great intelligence, grace and style.

It is obvious that I loved my REDKEN life and my world became my significant other. It was love that did not let me go. That's not exactly the theme of my life in relationships. Love did let me go, over and over.

There were meaningful relationships with wonderful men of a variety of careers including a colleague, a salon owner, a professional dancer, a business executive, a physician and a magician! The lifespan was between 1 year and 6 years. The majority of them were long-distance due to my insatiable need to be able to control the time we were able to spend together and being the one to leave rather than being the one to have been left.

With all the personal shock and material loss I had experienced, plus the loss of these relationships, I could honestly say, "I'm done!" I was newly and early retired from REDKEN with no focus or plan for how I would live out my golden years. One thing I did know, there would be no more opening of my heart to romantic entanglements.

I was D O N E!

However closed my heart was, I was determined it wouldn't turn into a heart of stone. This is a scriptural concept as well as a physiological one.

The physiological awareness began when I discovered HeartMath LLC at the Spirit in Business Conference in San Francisco in 2002.

My first training at the Boulder Creek, CA headquarters, HeartMath's heart and science convinced me that we could empower people to greatly reduce stress, build resilience and unlock their natural intuitive guidance for making better choices.

It was my exposure here that convinced me this was REDKEN's method to "spoil our best customers."

I took the training to our salon professionals, over 2,500 of them, incorporating their heart's intelligence into their day-to-day experience of life and their pursuit of personal growth and better health.

After several years of teaching and practicing HeartMath's Quick Coherence, it was time that I enrolled in a weekly phone-in course entitled "Heart Relationships" to focus on my own 'heart of flesh.'

Our six-week course was hosted by trainer, Sheva Carr the founder of the HeartMastery Program through Fyeral Foundation. Sheva is an expert in accessing the heart's intelligence, receiving the benefits of the heart's impact on consciousness, health, performance and creativity.

I was about to discover Sheva would demonstrate loving-kindness and intelligence on every call.

We began on the first Wednesday with the introduction of the course and the expectation for the next five weeks. We were encouraged to participate, share our experiences and put action to the homework.

Within the first couple of weeks, Sheva gave us an assignment to write a daily sticky-note and leave them where our loved ones would find them. Each note would describe one reason, that day, we loved that person.

"Uh, Sheva," I spoke up, "I don't have a spouse or significant other." Sheva didn't hesitate. "Can you envision the person you would love to open your heart to and write the sticky-notes to that imaginary person?"

"Sure, I'll do that."

Each day, throughout the next thirty days of August, and on into September I wrote my sticky-notes to my imaginary love and stuck them on the pages of my journal.

My notes included messages such as:

- ❖ I love you when you call me or contact me and tell me how much I mean to you.
- ❖ I love your broad beautiful smile especially when you're enjoying a hardy, healthy laugh.
- ❖ I love you for the freedom you give me yet always let me know you're here for me.
- ❖ I love your appreciation of great music, of all genres, and your beautiful voice both singing and speaking.
- ❖ I love you for being willing to trust totally on God's love, will and provision using the gifts He's given in productive and serving ways.
- ❖ I love how you take care of your body, conscious of its physical needs to be fed healthy food, to move and build in healthy ways and to rest fully and completely each night.
- ❖ I love to hear you pray.

I wrote the sticky notes from August 6th through all the way through the month of September. Even while I was defining this partner I was declaring 'relationships are an add-on' and 'I don't want or need one,' I sensed God's voice, yet once again, during the night.

"If you think what you've accomplished is a big deal, you haven't seen anything yet, but I need for you to live a pure life."

I hadn't seen anything yet?

All I could do was reflect on all those accolades that I had received in the way of industry honors and awards.

I recalled the chapter entitled, "The Priestess of Profit" that author Patricia Aburdene wrote of me in her book <u>Megatrends 2010: The Rise of Conscious Capitalism</u>. In his book, <u>Living Brands,</u> Raymond Nadeau included me in a short list of corporate leaders who proved that companies could indeed have 'corporate soul.' And finally, in his book <u>Great Business Teams: Cracking the Code for</u> <u>Standout Performance,</u> Howard Guttman named the REDKEN senior management team, headed by our unsurpassed leader, Pat Parenty, as a model of corporate transformation to flat line management resulting in double digit profit for ten years consecutively.

Now I was being admonished by the Lord to look at these accomplishments and understand that "I hadn't seen anything yet." I was beyond curious to know what that meant.

From that dream night forward, I began to ask in my prayer and meditation time, "Ok Lord, what is pure for me? Pure for my body, mind, relationships, finances, spirit? All five points of my star?" I became more mindful of how I was feeding, watering and resting my body, capturing my thoughts, paying more attention to listening and loving my relationships, recording how much money "spilled" through my fingers, and finding time to "be still and know that He is God."

On a Saturday around noon in New York City, I was sitting at my round table in my apartment, "The Pod" and a Facebook message showed up on my computer screen from Rebecca Jetton.

"Rebecca Jetton?" I said out loud. "I don't know Rebecca Jetton. I know Max Jetton, maybe Rebecca's his sister. Maybe something happened to Max. But why would she be contacting me? I haven't seen Max since college, except for the few minutes at our 40th college class reunion that we'd attended the November before."

As a member of the Southern Nazarene University Alumni Board, I was actively engaged in the events surrounding Homecoming of 2010, the 40th anniversary of my college class. I was invited to be the MC of the luncheon where sixty of our former classmates were scheduled to attend. Max and Rebecca Jetton were invited by the University to accept the "Hall of Witnesses" award given by the religion department for faithful service in ministry during the same Homecoming weekend.

Following the award ceremony, Rebecca returned to their hotel room to rest, the effects of her cancer treatment stealing energy every moment. Max made his way to our class reunion luncheon. It was during our sharing time, he came forward to tell the story of his early remembrance of the campus. He was five years old and his parents, ministers of the Nazarene church in North Little Rock, brought a group of teens to the college to explore the possibilities of attending there.

Climbing up the stairs of the administration building and holding onto his mother's hand, he recalled her saying, "Just think Max, one day you might come to college here, too!" He affirmed in that moment he would attend Bethany Nazarene College.

I was moved by the story and when he headed back to his table I simply asked, "Could I have a hug?"

20
Manhattan To Molalla
A Journey Of Faith And Love

Fast forward now nearly a year later, sitting in my apartment, reading the email that was not from Rebecca, but from Max himself. Here, in his own words, is his story:

I was all alone. My youngest son, 12-year old Isaac, was spending the weekend with Ashley, his older sister's family, and I was feeling the loss of my wife's death more than ever. Three months earlier my wife, Rebecca, had lost her valiant seven year fight with stage four breast cancer which we had grieved every day of those seven years. I was alone.

Then I heard a familiar whisper, a mental impression which I believe was the Holy Spirit: "Rebecca's not coming back Max. You need to go on with your life."

"What does that mean Lord?" I took my wedding ring off and placed it on the night stand. "What does that mean Lord? What's next?"

I thought about reaching out to someone with whom I could relate my pain. I had a small group of men who had been with me during Rebecca's illness, now I had another group of guys who were helping me cope with my new life without her.

But I wondered if I could reach out and have a feminine ear to my pain. I wondered about someone from a previous pastorate or locale. I even thought about an online method of reaching out to find a caring response. Nothing or no one seemed right and I finally drifted off to an unsettled slumber.

The next morning, Saturday, September 24th, I awoke to a question from that familiar Voice. "What about that lady who was the emcee at your 40th college class reunion?"

"But Lord, I don't know her. We never had a conversation in the four years at school. I knew who she was and she knew my name but we didn't know each other. I don't know if she's married, in a relationship, or even where she lives. I don't even know how to spell her last name. Was it Mincy, Mincie, Mincey?"

So I Googled her. Let's see...Mincey. There she is. Let's see...Manhattan. Hmm...that's not the Little Apple (Manhattan, Kansas) either. Let's see...oh, Vice President of Global Communication for REDKEN of Fifth Avenue. Wow! I'm not sure that someone from Manhattan New York would be interested in someone from Molalla, Oregon.

Only after mustering up some courage and reassurances from within did I begin to write on the Facebook page with my family's picture as the wallpaper.

"Ann, my name is Max Jetton. My wife of 43 years recently died with breast cancer. We had a wonderful marriage, three children and five grandchildren. I just wanted someone with whom I could talk. At our 40th reunion you seemed to be a kind, caring and understanding person. Would you be available for a visit?"

Later that day I received a reply from Ann.

"Dear Max, I am an independent woman who walks alone on the planet. I am sorry about the loss of your bride. You have my condolences"

I don't remember the middle part of her reply, but I do remember the ending phrase: "If there's anything I can do I am here for you."

I wrote her back immediately and simply said, "I'll take you up on that last part."

The next day was Sunday and knowing the busyness of a pastor on Sunday, through email we made a date to speak on Monday before Max took Isaac to school.

Monday came and we spoke for an hour each sharing our life stories. I immediately related to his loss of his wife having suffered loss of my own loved ones, his life in the pastorate having grown up a preacher's kid, but frankly what I couldn't relate to was his life as a parent. I never was a mom.

Our compatibility was palpable even from afar. We knew we needed to make some kind of plan to see each other in the not-too-distant-future. It was in those first days of talking to each other that I suggested we return to our SNU for Homecoming that was approaching in November.

Before Homecoming arrived, I had been with Paula for a few days in October in preparation for the 50th Anniversary of REDKEN event she was hosting at the Beverly Hills Hotel. All of our 1993 pre-acquisition employees were invited to reunite in December.

Since I was already on the west coast, I emailed Max and told him I had a couple of days I could fly up to Portland and take him out for his upcoming birthday lunch. I didn't want to take for granted he would have time in his schedule. I simply asked if it would be possible.

He immediately wrote back kiddingly affirming he'd "check his calendar" to see if he could 'fit me in.'

I flew up on Sunday, October 31st, and arrived at PDX in the evening. Isaac was with Ashley and family trick-or-treating giving Max the available hours to come to the airport to greet me.

I walked through security looking to the right and seeing him in the reflection of the bullet-proof plexi-glass partition. He was actually to my left and when we finally met he took me in his safe and secure arms and said, "Welcome home."

As engraved in a gorgeous piece of granite in the Birmingham, AL airport, this description of home was what I felt in that moment.

"Home, a hearth where the spirit basks in warmth. A song humming softly. A lighted lamp and a welcome. It is a place to be glad in."

I was home.

We were beyond joyful to see each other, could hardly get all the words spoken that we had rehearsed to say in that moment. We made our way to my hotel on the airport grounds, said goodnight and made plans for our one day together beginning the next morning.

The next morning couldn't come quickly enough. He was right on time at 9:00 a.m. and we sat in the lobby of the hotel, had coffee, talked more and then left for our adventuresome day. As we were walking out to the car he spun me around spontaneous spoke these words, "Will you marry me?"

"Yes!" I responded. That quickly. That simply. That assuredly. "Yes." Then he clinched it for me when he looked me eye to eye and said, "God wants to love you through me."

What girl could ever refuse a proposal like that? It's scriptural that a "husband is to love his wife as Christ loved the church and gave himself for her." (Ephesians 5:25) Max was committing to do this for me. It had to be one of those "you haven't seen anything yet" promises God had meant for me in the August dream.

For the balance of that magical day we drove around beautiful Portland, visited Multnomah Falls, lunched at what has become now our signature restaurant The Chart House, and strolled through an October-barren famous Rose Garden overlooking the city. In the far distance stood the beauties Mt. Hood and Mt. Saint Helens.

I smiled to myself throughout the day. Portland was the very city where I received that first spiritual calling through Luke 4:17 and declared then and there that "I didn't want to be in the ministry." Now here I was, back in Portland with a man who would draw me into the ministry by drawing me to himself. God will have His way in His time. Or as Paula quoted, "Everything that should come to you will come to you through open and winding passages."

Following that first twenty-four hours together we knew we needed to spend more time and the idea of the Homecoming road trip needed to become a reality. However, as a pastor, it wasn't that easy for Max to just get away, take a Sunday off, and find someone available to fill the pulpit, but he did it.

Max made the plan for us to meet in Kansas City where he had family, sister Billie Lee and her husband Richard, and I had great lifelong friends Brad and Laura Moore. We'd meet there, stay with our respective connections and then hit the road for the 6 hour trip to Oklahoma City.

The weekend was surreal, returning to the school where we spent four years together yet apart. So near and yet so far. He was always in the religion department, I was in the gym. All of our friends embraced us, and we embraced each other.

Dr. David McKellips, the superintendent of Northeastern Oklahoma district has been one of Max's closest friends and allies. He met Max for breakfast during the weekend and implored him to "take his time with this new relationship." Dave also made the suggestion that one of us make a move so that we could experience the "dailies" of life and not continue as a long-distance relationship.

When Max suggested to me the idea of moving to Molalla there was not even a moment of hesitation, but rather complete assuredness that this is what I must do. There was no doubt. I would pack up New York City my city of 8,000,000 on the Atlantic and relocate to Molalla a city of 8,000 on the Pacific.

In addition to the inevitability of becoming a pastor's wife, the other eventuality was becoming a mother and grandmother. Never having children of my own, and when I was 24 years old having my tubes tied to assure that I wouldn't become a mom, I just couldn't relate to stepping into a ready-made, blended family. The Lord had different ideas.

In late December of 2010, I made the move into a new Molalla apartment complex which Max had prepared for me. Complete with furniture, linens, a coffee pot and blender, I was able to settle in quickly and easily. And we made a date for his family to come to his home for New Year's Day dinner.

Todd, his elder son, who was two days old when he was adopted by Max and Rebecca, arrived with his beautiful wife Sabrina and their two children Miles and Mia. Max's lovely natural daughter Ashley and her husband Justin arrived with their children Kenesaw, Zane and Soshie.

Isaac, his 12-year old descended the stairs when the doorbell rang. He loved spending time with his brother, sister and his nephews and nieces. All of them were still grieving the loss of their mother. And adjusting to a new woman in their father's life.

That first gathering was warm and welcoming with the daughters taking command of the kitchen doing what they do best. It was all comfy until Max broached the subject of our getting married. The energy of the room changed, Todd excused himself from the table. The reality of our desires and the needs of his family came head-to-head. It wasn't until after they said goodnight and we heard from Ashley in a text, that it was just too soon. They needed for us to rethink our March date and push it back to later in the year.

They were right. Although postponing our date was not our first choice we considered the sensitivity of what the family was experiencing. Quickly we chose to push our wedding date to June 25th exactly nine months from the date of our first email contact.

Ashley openly shared, "The grief I have for my mother has nothing to do with the joy I have for my father."

And Todd, after some time, shared with me that "the family wanted to know you were who you claimed to be. Now we know you are who you are and we're so glad to have you in our family." His words brought tears to my eyes.

In the meantime, I became involved with the activities of the church. Although not yet their official pastor's wife, I was right by Max's side in the first communion service, was interviewed by the local <u>Molalla Pioneer</u> newspaper on my move in an article entitled <u>Manhattan to Molalla: A Journey of Faith and Love</u>, and I accepted Max's invitation to speak in the Sunday morning service to introduce myself to the congregation.

After attending my first Bible Study, I was invited to become the Director of our Women's Ministries. I didn't know the first thing about Women's Ministries until it dawned on me that I'd been involved with women in my business all my career. We built a great team of women with amazing talent and gifts, women who were just waiting to be called upon to lead and serve. Starting with a group of 40 we built it to a group of 100. I was having the time of my life and was beginning to understand what the Lord had said in the dream, "You haven't seen anything yet!"

On June 25th, 2011 I walked down the aisle in our sanctuary to the sound of Max singing John Denver's "Annie's Song." In that glittering moment, with what I had experienced and observed in the months we had known each other, I realized Max fulfilled not just one, but all of the "sticky notes" I had written describing my imaginary true love.

The congregation stood as I approached him on the platform where he was surrounded by my family; sisters Jan and Cathy, nieces Heather, Lesley, Shannon and Jenice, best friend Marcia, my cousin Don and Joanne Dickerson. Husbands were there, too, Mike, Yannick, Don.

On Max's side were Todd and Sabrina, Ashley and Justin, Kenesaw and Isaac, Max's sister Bonnie. Then there were the children, Miles, Mia, Zane and Soshie and my great-niece Elyse.

Additionally, it took four, count them, four elders of the Church of the Nazarene to attend and bless our nuptials: Dr. David McKellips, Dr. Stan Reeder, Dr. Carl Clendenen and Rev. Doug Brumbaugh.

Our wedding didn't come without tragedy and last minute juggling. Our major planner, Chelle Watt, was busy in the fellowship hall of the church on rehearsal day finishing all the floral arrangements. She used her leg to move a table and immediately fell to the floor. Her weakened and vulnerable back gave way and she was immediately airlifted to Oregon Health & Sciences University to be tended to by the experts in spinal breaks.

My friends Linda Fender, Brenda Rydzewski, Eleanor Eyman along with Robin the owner of The Wild Iris Florist in Molalla finished the flowers, all the centerpieces, platform presentation bouquets, the bridal party's bouquets, boutonnieres, and my bouquet. I'll always be indebted to them for their willingness to be angels of mercy.

Our reception hosted a beautiful afternoon tea in the completely white pipe-and-draped gymnasium which one of our members described as

"Ann brought Manhattan to Molalla with these decorations" and Mrs. Clendenen said, "It must have cost you a fortune to hang all those sheets in the gym."

We changed out of our wedding clothes, said goodbye to family and friends (no rice, please) to begin our journey to the coast for a few days of honeymoon. On the way out of town I turned to Max and mustered up the courage to say, "Honey, I think we need to stop by OHSU and see how Chelle's doing, I want to leave my wedding bouquet with her."

The look on his newlywed face was classic. "Really?" was all it conveyed. "Really, is that what you want to do right now?"

"Yes, it is." And so we stopped, found Chelle with Steve, her dedicated husband. She was sedated and was barely able to open her eyes and utter the words, "So sorry Annie, I didn't get to finish your flowers." I laid my bridal bouquet on the bed next to her, kissed her cheek and told her to focus on complete healing.

Oh we made it to the coast for two glorious days of "getting to know you," then on to Arkansas to meet the folks, finally completing the whole honeymoon dream in St. Thomas compliments of our friends Peter and Beverly Millard. Bliss!

I got married, became a mother (and grandmother) and got my Medicare card all in the same year.

Officially I became a pastor's wife and enjoyed loving our "flock" right along with Max. We had two and a half years, right up to his retirement in May of 2013. Our retirement service was a beautiful exclamation point on Max's 45 years in ministry. Speeches included Todd and Ashley as well as members of the church board representing the congregation. They offered a variety of gifts and hosted a lavish luncheon with perfectly appointed décor.

Max cleared out the final bins from his church study and drove away. He was done.

He had finished the race, he had kept the faith. And now it was time for him to rest. It was through these days and years that I was learning to be a mother. Max and I were blissful newlyweds and knew it was important for us as to include our now 13-year old son, Isaac in our plans and activities as a family.

21
Isaac's Story
The Second Divinely Appointed Adoption

His story represents their second Divinely appointed adoption that the Jetton's felt was God's will.

It was June 7th, 1997, a baby was born to a young woman in Romania, a country that was ruled by a notorious dictator. For years the ruthless leader had declared birth control outlawed in order that the country could be populated quickly.

Never mind that he had also depleted the country of employment and opportunities to feed their families.

The young woman made her way across the country from her hometown to Arad, a western-most city near the Hungarian border, found the Spitalul Clinic de Obstetrica Si Ginecolgoie Maternity Hospital and in due time, delivered the baby boy, "born on term from a pregnancy with normal evolution by a spontaneous birth."

Hospital administrators gathered information solely from the mother's verbal declaration as she had no documents of identification. She gave her name and the name of the boy's father who did not legally recognize the newborn. She also provided information on their current residence.

No further data was collected. The mother abandoned the child immediately after birth and left, never to return. No family members came to check on the baby.

The information provided was erroneous.

There he was, baby boy all alone, declared legally abandoned by the Law Court of the Arad municipality.

Alone that is, until a kind, compassionate social worker was Divinely drawn to the little guy. She was in her mid-twenties, married, and was observing the testing of little Catalain in his early months of development.

Camelia fell in love with Catalain. Although married, she didn't have children of her own so he filled that void within her heart. She would bring him toys, socks with cartoon characters on them, and changes of clothes. She held him, took him out into the sunshine, simply showing loving care to the little one.

Out of the 300 children housed in the Placement Center #1 the Associate Misionare Crestine "Betleem", (just one of many orphanages in the country at the time) Catalain was her favorite child.

A world away in Broken Arrow, Oklahoma, Max and Rebecca Jetton were pastors of the Church of the Nazarene and parents of two grown children Todd and Ashley. Rebecca taught in the public school system. She was moved by the story of her fellow teachers who had adopted an orphan from one of those Romanian orphanages.

So moved was she that she presented the idea of adopting a Romanian child. Max was 50-years old which meant he would be raising a teenager during his golden years.

They were notified by the Romanian authorities and through a series of video introductions they made their choice. They were going to travel to Bucharest, meet with Camelia, and bring little Catalain to America. Here he would receive overwhelming love and nourishment from his new parents, family, and church family. He would be able to go to school, play sports, develop friendships.

Most of all, Catalain would have the opportunity to hear the story of Jesus' love and to make a decision to commit his life to Him.

First order of business, Catalain Maris, was named Isaac Thomas Jetton. His name comes from the Old Testament, "Isaac" the son of Abraham and Sarah who was born at their advanced ages of 100 and 85, which prompted the name because it's meaning is "child of laughter."

Now at 21-months old, Isaac's Romanian passport was exchanged for a US passport, but not before the judge in Oklahoma City turned to Isaac and said, "I believe you're old enough to repeat after me," asked Isaac to raise his little right hand, and began to quote the Naturalization Oath of Allegiance.

Imagine Isaac, not yet two-years old, repeating these words:

"I hereby declare, on oath, that I absolutely and entirely renounce and abjure all allegiance and fidelity to any foreign prince, potentate, state, or sovereignty, of whom or which I have heretofore been a subject or citizen...so help me God."

Fast-forward sixteen years.

The Jetton's had moved to Oregon to take an executive pastorate position in Beaverton a suburb of Portland very near Todd and Ashley. Rebecca discovered just before the move, a lump in her breast and after seven years with stage four cancer, she passed away.

On the day she died, the movers were at their home in Beaverton preparing to move Max and Isaac to Molalla a small cattle and timber town southeast of the City.

Max made connections with and found support from pastors in Molalla by attending a monthly pastors' luncheon. One such man was the pastor of the local Seventh Day Adventist Church. Pastor Eddie is a native Romanian and in a conversation one day, Max casually mentioned Isaac's story and Pastor Eddie volunteered help to locate Camelia Palcu, the social worker from the Romanian orphanage.

It was Max's understanding that Camelia attended an Adventist Church in Arad. Surprisingly, Pastor Eddie responded positively, saying he would make contact with his pastor friends there and let him know when they made connection.

It happened.

Max received a Facebook message from Camelia who was beyond overjoyed to hear from him and Isaac after all these years. She had relocated with her husband to Barcelona, left her work with children and social services, and found employment in the duty free store in the Barcelona airport.

It was a pure miracle that the Adventist pastor was able to find her. It was not Camelia who was a member of his local church, it was a former colleague and friend from the orphanage who knew where to find Camelia.

Max had always promised Isaac that he would, one day, return him to Romania to see and hear, feel and taste his home country. Not knowing how it would all come together, he kept that promise in his heart. So, the summer of 2015, at the completion of Isaac's junior year of high school, we boarded a flight from Portland to Bucharest.

Camelia was disappointed knowing that we would be visiting Romania and she would miss us. However, she was thrilled with having email and Facebook to keep in touch.

We made our plans and began to plot our travel within the country, sight-seeing on the coast and the castles all the details to support ten days away from home. Amazingly we heard from Camelia. Her brother's child was scheduled to be christened the weekend we would be in Arad. She rearranged her dates to travel in for the family event and included extra days to make it possible to come while we were in town.

In a rental car with Max at the helm and Isaac his GPS co-pilot, we wound our way throughout the country's mountains, the flat farmlands, and finally arrived in Arad. On Sunday afternoon a taxi pulled up to the entrance of our hotel and a small, sweetly smiling lady emerged from the backseat carrying a gift in a plastic bag from the Barcelona duty free shop.

Max met her first, giving her a welcome hug. He then turned to his son, and said, "And here's Isaac."

Unfathomable, that moment of recognition of connection and gratitude. That moment held all the emotion imaginable of two people who had been separated sixteen years earlier and now they were together.

They laughed. They hugged.

We made our way up to our suite and listened to story after story as Camelia spoke in lovely English her recollection of what life was like for the children in the orphanage under the dictatorship. She offered her gift to Isaac.....chocolate! His favorite.

Then she reached into her purse and brought out a handful of photos from Isaac's earliest days, photos we had never seen. The ultimate was a birthday card she had sent him for his third birthday. The only address she had was Broken Arrow but since the Jetton's had moved to a new pastorate in California, the card was returned to her in Arad.

For sixteen years she kept the card. For sixteen years she prayed every single day that one day God would arrange for her to see Catalain, now Isaac, once again. She gave him the card and the photos. He smiled.

He was home.

Within just three blocks of our downtown Arad hotel still stood the Maternity Hospital and the orphanage. In the beauty of the sunshine we walked and talked, took photos and listened to stories until we arrived at the two buildings. We heard the precious quivers of babies' cries, the hospital still actively providing a safe place for children to be born. The other was now eerily empty, the orphanage.

Of all the children for which Camelia was responsible while she served as social worker, the one and only child she's ever seen again was this child...her favorite....her Catalain, our Isaac.

Living with Isaac, through the development ages 13 to 18, taught me that teenagers can be compliant, they can respect their parents, they can enjoy family gatherings, they can accept guidance, they can have values that help them make the right decisions. Oh yes, they can do all that while they are realizing and creating their own independence, their own friend circles, their own interests and career choices.

Isaac has taught me that we can, yes even teenagers can, live as Jesus taught; to be in the present moment, not worry about yesterday nor tomorrow; be observant and believe the best of people, don't rush to judgment, withhold criticism, be cautious.

His high school years have been combined with community college study resulting in a diploma and associates of arts degree in one graduation season. Going forward to university, his plan to graduate in Criminal Justice will be completed in two years and soon enough he'll find himself as a law enforcement officer, "getting the bad guys off the street."

Truly Isaac has been one of those "you haven't seen anything yet" the Lord promised in the dream.

22
The Double Life Of The Pastor's Wife

Through all my days of being pastor's wife, step-mother and grandmother (Grannie Annie or Nana Anna), my work with REDKEN has gone forward. The thought, "if the work comes to me, it's my work to do" continued to be my mantra and I honor it to this day. When the company calls and invites me to speak with the intention of "spoiling our best salon customers" or to train new sales consultants on the REDKEN story, I don't hesitate, I answer with an enthusiastic 'yes!'

My greatest treasure now is when I can share what we've built and pass the torch to the next generation, and in one instance, to our daughter-in-law Sabrina. She was contracted by Entia Biosciences to brand their exclusive line of hair and skin care products based on amino acid ergothioneine and vitamin D2. Sabrina developed the packaging and the certification education online for salon professionals resulting in the brand getting the attention of the senior management team of L'Oreal Professional Products division.

Sabrina made a trip to New York with Dr. Marvin Hausman the medical doctor who created the innovative way to use mushrooms under ultraviolet light to produce the combination of ergothioneine and vitamin D2. They presented the products and all the support materials.

The L'Oreal management team were highly complementary and accepted the presentation and the product offering as it was, no changes. Sabrina and Dr. Hausman were beyond gratified.

Just prior to the meeting closing Sabrina spoke up one final time. "Before we adjourn, I wanted to bring greetings from Oregon and Ann Mincey."

To understand the shift of energy in the moment is to understand that included among the attendees around the table were a few of my colleagues on that tight-knit REDKEN senior management team. Pat Parenty, Karen Fuss-Zipp, Christine Schuster.

Startled, Pat spoke up, "How do you know Ann Mincey?"

Sabrina smiled and responded, "She's my mother-in-law."

The room went wild.

I often refer to my life as "The double life of the pastor's wife" as I keep one foot in a fashionable stiletto and the other in a rubber cowboy boot.

I continue to be an independent woman however I no longer have to walk alone on the planet.

Epilogue

Each morning Max and I have established our time, whether together or separated by my travels on the road, to begin our day in prayer. He prays first always in the spirit of gratitude for our life and love, our family and church families. He'll include immediate needs of those we love and he's so good to include his gratitude to the Lord for me.

My prayer follows with my own list of gratitude's; our health, our sound minds, our loving relationships, our finances and our connection to God. The five points of the star. I pray for my family, one by one by name asking for protection and provision. I lift up my closest friends and their concerns and close by thanking the Lord for Max and his commitment to "allowing You (God) to love me through him."

I lead us into reciting the Lord's Prayer by saying, "we offer our prayers in the name of Jesus and pray the prayer he taught us, the prayer He actually prayed." At the end of this session of prayer, we then focus on the day and get on with our individual and partnered activities.

Beginning our day in this sacred space sets the tone, helps us to do as the scriptures admonish, "…..to rejoice and be glad in it." Ending each day with Isaac in the "dailies" review and prayer puts the bookends of our day in peaceful perspective.

In addition to our time together, it is my practice to spend quiet time reading, journaling and meditating all alone. It is during these moments that I reach for a prayer book, <u>Lean Back on the Everlasting Arms</u> containing the transcribed prayers of Dr. Kenneth O. Jones the Associate Minister of The Fifth Avenue Presbyterian Church where I worshipped while in New York City. Although now deceased, Dr. Jones' prayers, continue to speak to my heart as I imagine him in the pulpit with his long gray robe and his kind generous face praying in his glorious Welsh voice. It was always as if God Himself was praying through him. He possessed the rare gift to lift his congregation, including me, into the very presence of God with prayers that were always tailored made to our needs. Regardless of the state of my heart and mind when entering the sacred sanctuary, I always left uplifted, encouraged, and inspired by Dr. Jones' prayers.

Reviewing some of my favorite passages that I've underlined in my dog-eared book now severed from its binding and having survived 21 years of packing and unpacking since I first began reading it, I offer them here to you. Please note how these lines of peace and grace reflect the contents of **Illuminate Radiate Resonate.**

"….we are sons and daughters of the King, and may claim our inheritance of new life, of grace unbounded, of love without measure."

"And we give thanks for our own loved ones and dear friends, who have blessed us with nurture and confidence and love. May their memorial be in our hearts in a special way this day. And we give thanks for the privilege of the remembrance of things past, for the tenderness of association and affection which balance the harshness of life. Keep us ever sensitive to these emotional responses, and never let us be ashamed of the sentiments of the heart or the mental rehearsal of loving relationships."

"….Through heart, spirit, emotions, mind, O God, we await the ministry of thy healing love, and the silent therapy of Thy grace and forgiveness."

"And so we pray for health - in body and mind, in emotion and spirit. We pray for health that is salvation - being put together again - being made whole - finding ourselves functioning in synchronized harmony, feeling once again that our aspirations and our realistic estimates are coming closer together. It is for this recovery of wholeness we pray, O God. For this Thou hast created, us. Thou hast put Christ as the energy of Thy Spirit to renew and empower us."

"Help us, O God, as people of faith and spiritual discernment, help us to demonstrate the beauty of the things that are true and lovely and of good report. In a day when the mediocre seems accepted as the norm, help us to remember that we follow our Lord Jesus, who called us to excellence, to a higher goal, to a vision of perfection. May we stand firm in our respect for relationships, for sacred matters, for the process of aging, for love and sex and beauty and friendship. May we not just become critics of all that is tawdry and trivial, but seek to be those who reach toward creativity and beauty and strive to restore in each person the glory of the Divine image."

It is my prayer that you have discovered in the story details contained here, the very real presence, voice and guidance of God.

His promise is we can **Illuminate** because "we are the light of the world." He has proven true for more than a century through my family heritage and in my childhood as a preacher's kid.

His presence, voice and guidance have proven we can **Radiate** because "we are a star right where we are." He has proven this throughout a career that dispelled the 'lie of comparisons' and promoted a life lived in balanced and resilient joy.

And finally, after wandering around the "desert" for 40 years with all the accomplishments, my full circle return home, His presence, voice and guidance has proven true that we can **Resonate** because "we are a true work of heart."

Great-grandfather Thomas Jefferson Poole, walking his field as he held on to the reins of the two work horses as they pulled a crude old plow was heard singing at the top of his voice:

> *"It is for us all today, if we trust and truly pray;*
> *Consecrate to Christ your all, and upon the Savior call,*
> *Praise God! It is for us all today!"*

God's presence, voice and guidance is for us all, today. Start your own adventure, no matter where you are in your life stage, and make the choice to **Illuminate**, **Radiate** and **Resonate**.

"You haven't seen anything yet!